Hand Lettering for Happiness

An Introduction to Hand Lettering &
Calligraphy Techniques—Designed to Spark Joy!

BRENNA JORDAN

Author of *The Lost Art of Handwriting*

Adams Media
New York   London   Toronto   Sydney   New Delhi

Adams Media
An Imprint of Simon & Schuster, Inc.
100 Technology Center Drive
Stoughton, Massachusetts 02072

First Adams Media trade paperback edition November 2023

ADAMS MEDIA and colophon are registered trademarks of Simon & Schuster, Inc.

For information about special discounts for bulk purchases, please contact Simon & Schuster Special Sales at 1-866-506-1949 or business@simonandschuster.com.

The Simon & Schuster Speakers Bureau can bring authors to your live event. For more information or to book an event, contact the Simon & Schuster Speakers Bureau at 1-866-248-3049 or visit our website at www.simonspeakers.com.

Interior design by Colleen Cunningham
Handwriting samples by Brenna Jordan
Interior images © 123RF/Daria Dombrovskaya, goodstudio; Getty Images/Mashot

Manufactured in the United States of America

10 9 8 7 6 5 4 3 2 1

Library of Congress Cataloging-in-Publication Data has been applied for.

ISBN 978-1-5072-2100-6

Hi, friend,

This book is dedicated to you. Whatever level you are at, you are invited to join this hand lettering celebration! These pages will meet you right where you are and guide you to take what you learn and craft your own original style. My hope is that this book brings you immense joy each time you pick up your pen to create and that the words in the quotes and affirmations make you happy to be you.

Happy writing!

Brenna

You ARE Made FOR Greatness

Contents

Introduction

Hand lettering is the act of thoughtfully shaping letters and designing eye-catching layouts in an unhurried, reflective way. It's a relaxing, joyful activity that is unique to every person. The very practice of hand lettering instills mindfulness and happiness, allowing you time to focus on how this art form sparks joy in you as you take pleasure in the beauty of your craft.

Hand lettering is not only a blissful experience—it's also good for your health! Modern neuroscience has uncovered physiological and emotional benefits to putting pen to paper, such as relieving stress, releasing dopamine (the "happiness chemical") in your brain, and boosting your memory. When you feel relaxed and engaged with an activity like hand lettering, you're more likely to find happiness. In *Hand Lettering for Happiness*, you will be introduced to tools and techniques that nurture your creativity and inspire joy.

- In **Part 1**, you'll learn about supplies and basic strokes you'll need to get started, and you'll discover several essential alphabets in both script and print.
- In **Part 2**, you'll find fifty quote and affirmation projects—all centered around happiness! As you write, you can focus on the meaning behind the quotes from historical figures, beloved authors, and film and television stars, and internalize the positive, joyful intent behind the affirmations. Each project will highlight a different aspect of hand lettering to practice as you copy the words. You'll also learn advanced aspects of hand lettering, such as how to combine multiple lettering styles, create banners, add special touches via flourishing, design illustrations, and so much more!
- In **Part 3**, you'll find framed pages on which you can create your own hand lettering projects. You can re-create projects you learned in Part 2 or come up with your own quote designs. Cut out your expertly handcrafted lettering projects and give them as gifts, or frame and hang them up in your home as reminders of your hard work and the happiness hand lettering brings you.

Hand Lettering for Happiness is intentionally designed to encourage calm, peaceful self-care time. As you practice writing the positive, uplifting words throughout this book, try to reflect on and absorb their meanings. Then let your finished projects continue to bring you happiness every time you see them!

The Basics of Hand Lettering

"Art flourishes where there is a sense of adventure."
—Alfred North Whitehead

Part 1 covers the basics of hand lettering, including the tools and materials you need to get started, as well as a few definitions to set you up for success on your lettering journey. You'll also find a variety of fun and exciting alphabets in both script and print that you will use throughout the book. You can reference these complete alphabets later for your own creative designs. Studying and practicing these foundational letters will provide a great base for you to begin observing and adding more styles to your collection. You may want to start a designated notebook just for gathering new ideas, as well as a practice notebook to gauge your progress.

As you dive into Part 1, you'll also discover practical step-by-step instructions for essential design, along with extensive troubleshooting advice to propel your calligraphy and lettering designs to the next level. Exploring creative entrance stroke options, flourishing strategies, and smaller building block activities will further prepare you for more advanced layouts.

As much as possible, try to follow the book in numerical order, since everything you work on in Part 1 has been carefully arranged to prepare you for the progressively more challenging projects in Part 2. In lettering, both the process and outcome hold many serendipitous twists and turns, so during your practice time, cultivate an atmosphere of adventure. Being curious about trying new techniques and styles will lead to both steady improvement and exciting self-discovery!

Tools and Materials

One of the best things about hand lettering is that you need very little equipment to get started, and basic materials are inexpensive and readily available.

Pencils

You'll want a good supply of your favorite pencils for practicing, doodling, and designing drafts. Some of my favorite pencils are Blackwing, Staedtler, and the GraphGear Pentel mechanical pencil, but any pencil that's comfortable for you will work! If you are left-handed, you'll want to use a pencil that has a high smudge resistance, such as the Uni Mitsubishi 9000.

Pens

It's important to practice using pens since these are the tools you will use whenever you make final designs. You will also be using them to work on anything that you want to be more formal or permanent, such as writing letters, addressing envelopes, and creating in your bullet journal. From very thin-line pens to thick brushstroke options, there's a style for whatever project you're working on.

BRUSH PENS

A brush pen has a flexible tip that uses pressure and release to form heavier downstrokes and lighter upstrokes for different calligraphy styles. There's a plethora of brush pens on the market, but you can't go wrong with the Tombow Fudenosuke, which comes in both a hard and soft tip. Besides these, the Pentel brush pen is a favorite, as is the Karin brush marker for when you want to make larger letters. All of these come in a variety of colors, and the Karin markers have an unparalleled set of metallic brush markers that are fantastic for special projects.

MONOLINE PENS

Monoline pens are different from brush pens and pointed pens because they have an inflexible tip that makes all their lines the same thickness. There are a ton of different types of monoline pens, but if you need something waterproof and smudge-proof, Microns are a good choice. You'll want to have a few different point thicknesses on hand so you can vary the weight of your letters. Paper Mate felt-tips are another type of monoline pen—they come in a huge variety of colors and are great for practicing.

POINTED PENS

Pointed pens are a classic alternative to the modern brush pens. They also have a flexible tip that uses the same pressure-and-release technique as brush pens. If you want an even slower and more meditative experience, as well as more control over your thick and thin lines, scripting with a pointed pen is an extraordinary endeavor that involves a penholder, nib, and ink for dipping. I highly recommend taking a class or workshop with a trained instructor, as the process is involved and expert guidance is invaluable. It's essential to try various nibs and penholders to see what works best for you. Everyone is different, and if you are more heavy-handed when you write, certain nibs, such as the Zebra G, will perform better. Be sure to use inks specially designed for pointed pens, such as:

- Moon Palace
- Pelikan
- Ziller
- Dr. Ph. Martin's Bleedproof White for writing on dark paper

You can also experiment with watercolor (liquid watercolor by Ecoline is my favorite) and gouache (Winsor & Newton and Schmincke are both good choices). Gouache is a thick pigment that comes in tubes in a wide variety of colors, which you squeeze onto your palette and mix with distilled water until you have the desired consistency. Gouache is perfect when you want to customize your colors and need brilliant and opaque coverage.

FOUNTAIN PENS

Fountain pens are another type of monoline pen. Like the pointed pen, they are traditional and elegant, dating back to an era when items could not be easily replaced. They are refillable with cartridges or ink, and, though not a necessity, they provide a luxurious writing experience. There's a wide range of choices, from very affordable to super spendy. If possible, try out fountain pens in a pen store before you make your selection so you can find what feels the best in your hand. You can use fountain pens for lettering and illustration, but they also function well in place of a ballpoint pen for anything handwritten.

Paper

You'll need a few different kinds of paper:

☐ First, get a **lined notebook** or **graph paper notebook** to practice the exercises in this book. Not only will your notebook allow you space for extra practice; you'll also have everything in one place to analyze your work, make improvements, and track your progress.

☐ **Tracing paper** is also great to have on hand, especially if you prefer not to write in the book.

☐ Whenever you use any brush pen, try to use **extra-smooth paper** so you don't fray your brush quickly. I recommend buying a Rhodia pad (or something comparable) or a large pack of HP Premium LaserJet paper for any brush pen practice you will be doing throughout this book. Bright white Canson Marker paper also works well—both for practicing and for making final designs that you want to scan and digitize.

☐ For projects requiring **fine art paper**, I recommend avoiding cold-press papers and sticking with a smooth Bristol, such as Strathmore or Canson, or another smooth variety such as Arches calligraphy paper.

☐ You can also be on the lookout for ways to salvage usable **scrap paper** from going in the trash. If it has a blank side, you can use it for your pencil design work and help save the environment as well!

☙ Maximize Practice Time

If you are debating
What to do while waiting
Why not try creating?

I wrote this little rhyme as a silly reminder for myself and my kids to pick up a pencil and doodle during those "bored moments" when it's typical to scroll on a device. You, too, can benefit from these spare minutes in waiting rooms, school parking lots, or during commercials: All are occasions to sneak in some stimulating lettering practice and boost your mood by choosing positive and encouraging words to write.

Other Supplies

There are optional supplies that you will appreciate having:

- [ ] **Gray brush pens** are awesome for shading your lettering.

- [ ] Prismacolor **colored pencils** are exceptional for adding vibrant color to both lettering and illustrations.

- [ ] If you like sparkles, the Wink of Stella **glitter brush marker** comes in a variety of colors to embellish your letters or illustrations—the brush tip provides a super-easy way to add a lovely shimmer.

- [ ] You might want some other **specialty pens**, such as Molotow liquid chrome, Uni Posca white, Pilot Parallel pens (broad-edged pens), Uniball silver and gold pens, Pentel sparkle pens, and the Permapaque (a permanent pen that's ideal for writing on wood or other surfaces and has no odor!).

- [ ] I like to have a variety of **erasers** on hand in different sizes and textures and in both black and white. My favorite for erasing final projects is the Tombow Mono Zero Elastomer Eraser. When you are erasing on dark paper, be sure to use a black eraser. A kneaded eraser is also great to have for delicate papers, and it leaves no residue.

- [ ] It's also optimal to have an assortment of **rulers**. I recommend keeping both clear and T-square rulers among your supplies.

- [ ] A few good **paintbrushes** in different sizes, mixing palettes, and pipettes (for adding water one drop at a time to thin gouache and ink) will also add to your art collection.

●✿ Write Down Your Favorite Words

If you read or hear a quote, song lyric, or idea that hits home, write it down immediately in a journal of quotes and excerpts (or in the Notes app on your phone in a pinch). It could be as short as a timely phrase a friend speaks or as long as a paragraph from a book. Writing it gives you time to reflect and helps it sink deeper into your memory. If it's really significant for you, develop it into a hand lettered design you can post on your fridge or bulletin board to read often.

A Few Definitions

- An **uppercase** letter is also called a capital letter or majuscule.

- A **lowercase** letter is also called a small letter or minuscule.

- In traditional writing, letters sit on a **base line**. Lowercase letters that are **x-height** (such as *x*, *c*, and *m*) extend to the mid line.

- **Ascenders** are the parts of lowercase letters that extend above the mid line to the ascender line. The seven ascender letters are *b*, *d*, *f*, *h*, *k*, *l*, and *t*, and they, along with descenders, provide perfect opportunities for flourishing!

- The **descenders** extend below the mid line to the descender line. There are seven descenders in script: *f*, *g*, *j*, *p*, *q*, *y*, and *z* (*f* and *z* are not descenders in print).

- **Counters** are the enclosed spaces within letters such as *A*, *a*, *O*, *o*, *e*, and *R*. They provide creative opportunities for veering from typical interpretation.

- **Entrance strokes** and **exit strokes** are the small, curved lines that lead to and from letters. They bring stability and elegance to letters and allow them to seamlessly join together.

- **Flourishes** are the dramatic lines extending from ascenders, descenders, cross bars, capital letters, and other features in a design that add interest and personality.

- **Ligatures** are formed when two or more letters join to make a more efficient or attractive symbol. Sometimes it looks cleaner to have a ligature for practical reasons, such as a double *t*-crossing. Other times, ligatures are used purely for reasons of aesthetics and creative expression.

- **Downstrokes** are thick strokes made by applying pressure with a brush, nib, or brush pen, while **upstrokes** are created by releasing pressure and using a light touch to achieve a delicate line.

Script Styles

Script consists of letters that are joined by entrance and exit strokes. Because of the rhythm and cadence of connecting letters, these styles contribute beauty, romance, and artistry to designs. Besides the charm of the letter forms, script is also a wonderful springboard for flourishing and adding other fun embellishments. Throughout the project pages, you'll start to notice creative opportunities available through script: weaving letters and words together in a kind of magic and expressing moods and ideas through how you write. Script alphabets also provide contrast in designs containing print styles.

BRUSH PEN WARM-UPS FOR SCRIPT STYLES

Brush pens allow you to vary the thicknesses of your strokes by applying pressure. Try practicing the brush pen strokes on the left-hand side of the next page. If you've never used a brush pen before, be patient with yourself! It takes practice to get used to the technique. Remember to apply firm, even pressure on the downstrokes, and lift up, as if on tiptoes, for the upstrokes. A light touch on these upstrokes will give you exquisite and graceful lines that are a beautiful contrast to the thick swells of the downstrokes.

Whenever you sit down to hand letter, it's a good idea to do warm-ups. Just a few minutes will help loosen your hand and allow your brain to get in the writing zone. This warm-up should feel meditative and leisurely, not rigid and strict. Here are ideas to get started:

➙ Benefits of Writing by Hand

Hand lettering engages your brain, body, mind, and emotions. Research shows that writing by hand stimulates the brain in more areas than typing does. A calming practice that helps express feelings and soothe anxieties, writing by hand can help boost both your mood and your memory, as well as improve learning and comprehension of whatever you are scripting. Best yet, you can make it a meaningful ritual that is customized to fit your needs and your schedule, and you can use your writing to beautify your space and bring happiness to others.

- Use a good-quality hard-tip brush pen for the best control.

- First, trace the lines and shapes, then make your own.

- Alternate thick and thin (downstrokes and upstrokes) to mimic writing letters.

Besides warming up with a brush pen, you can also warm up simply by practicing your handwriting. The biggest differences between cursive handwriting and brush script are the varying thicknesses that are possible with your flexible brush tip or nib and the slower speed that is required to execute brush script. However, monoline cursive and the bolder brush script each have an important place in both your practice and your designs. One easy exercise is to study letters whenever you can and notice the nuances of handwriting and brush script. You can observe both of these styles everywhere—in ads, signs, magazines, and even packaging at the grocery store.

Careful practice of cursive alphabets with a monoline tool (without the flexible brush tip) is one of the best preparations for writing in brush script. When you are happy with your letters in monoline, it will be much easier to add the extra dimension of using a tool with a flexible tip.

UPPERCASE CURSIVE ALPHABET

Here's one example of a basic uppercase cursive alphabet to compare with brush script. Take your time and re-create this alphabet slowly and rhythmically in your separate notebook with either a pencil or your favorite monoline pen.

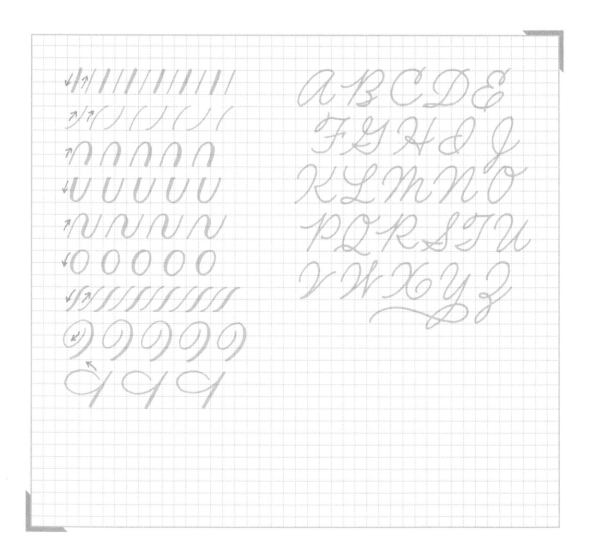

Copperplate Script

Copperplate script has stood the test of time. This fashionable calligraphy style, also called English Roundhand, originated in England hundreds of years ago but is still wildly popular today. The name Copperplate comes from the time-consuming process in which scribes wrote manuscripts and engravers meticulously etched them into copperplate (backward!) to be inked.

Once you start practicing Copperplate, you'll notice that this beautiful, flowing script is ubiquitous—on wedding invitations, logos, and home decor, just to name a few. Many calligraphers use a traditional pointed pen for Copperplate letters. While brush pens are easier and less messy to use and transport, there's an undeniable magic to crafting your letters with tools that take you back in time.

LOWERCASE COPPERPLATE

Trace these lowercase letters. Write as slowly as you can—but not so slowly that your lines start wobbling! Finding the right speed can be tricky, but slowing down a few more notches than you'd think is necessary will usually get the best results. The lowercase letters are generally easier than uppercase, so start here before moving on to capitals.

UPPERCASE COPPERPLATE

Now for the exciting capital letters! If you need guidance with the sequence of the strokes, trace the first sample letter following the directional arrows and/or numbers. Then trace the letter again. For further practice, keep working on each letter of the alphabet in your separate notebook. For every letter, aim to get at least three in a row that you're happy with before moving on to the next letter. Take a few moments to analyze your page, star your favorites, and notice where you can improve. This simple pause will give your brain time to file your successes for next time.

Once you feel fairly confident with both the lowercase and uppercase alphabets, tailor your practice to your own interests by writing words or names to get comfortable with all kinds of letter joins. It helps to go through the alphabet in order, writing whatever name or word comes to mind, starting each word with a capital letter. And remember to take breaks when you get tired, or you will find your work becoming less polished. Even with just a few minutes a day, you'll be surprised how quickly you will see improvement when you practice regularly!

Once you learn the basics of the traditional alphabet, the sky's your limit. There are endless possibilities for letter variations in both lowercase and uppercase. Like classic items in a wardrobe, the letters of this script can be elegantly simple or dressed up with dramatic accessories. The *E* at the end of the alphabet on the next page shows you what that might look like.

●◆ Spread Joy by Hand Lettering a Card

Want a practical and wholesome way to put your hand lettering to use? Make a "Thinking of You" card with one of the new lettering styles you've learned and send a note to someone. You'll find letter writing included on many lists of activities that increase happiness. And the greatest thing about letter writing? Besides making you happier, you'll also make someone else's day!

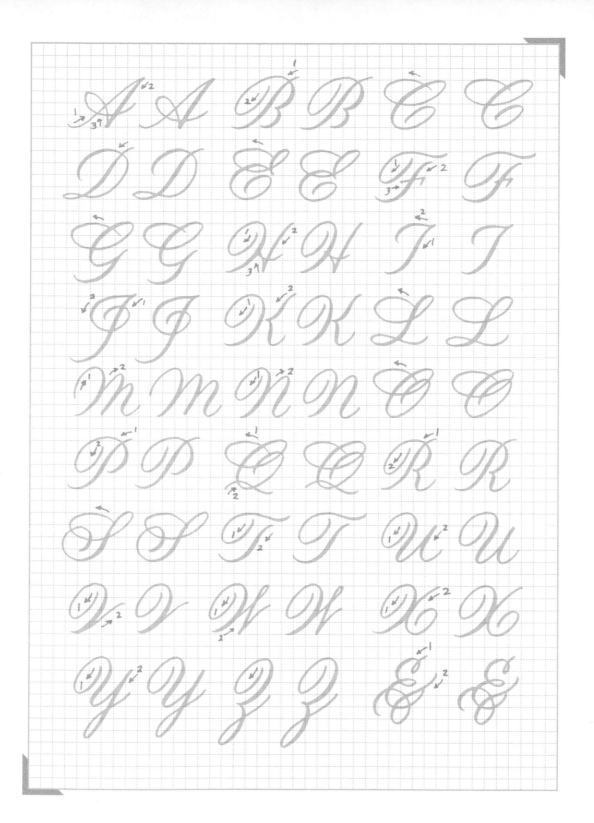

Spencerian Script

Spencerian script shares some similarities with Copperplate. Designed by Platts Rogers Spencer in the mid-1800s, this style was influenced by the natural beauty Spencer observed around his home, which he then infused into the letter forms. Based on the smooth ovals of stones on a lakeshore, the uppercase letters are ornate and can be heavily flourished, while the lowercase letters have a clean, simple, and angular look. Because the letters are spaced far apart, they are easy to read.

LOWERCASE SPENCERIAN

The lowercase letters were designed to be written more quickly than Copperplate, so they are mostly monoline in appearance, although shades can be added on certain letters if desired. Trace these lowercase letters first, remembering to keep a light touch. After tracing the samples, try making your own Spencerian letters.

UPPERCASE SPENCERIAN

Next, move on to the uppercase letters, following the sequence arrows on the first tracing sample before tracing the second. For Spencerian capital letters, the pressure on the downstrokes is applied differently than for the Copperplate uppercase. The downstroke begins without pressure until about the middle of the stroke, and then the bottom part of the stroke contains a thick swell. A few extra variations are introduced at the end of the alphabet.

Upbeat Script

If you're working on style selection for a design, take your time and think about what mood or image you'd like to express. When you need a modern style that doesn't come across as formal or traditional, this script creates a more laid-back appearance. Upbeat Script is a great choice when you want a style that's less fancy or loopy than more conventional script types. It also works well with a paintbrush. This script can portray a faster tempo if you are trying to get the meaning of speed across since these letters have fewer frills and flourishes garnishing the text.

LOWERCASE UPBEAT SCRIPT

These Upbeat Script lowercase letters exhibit strength with their quick, confident strokes. Feel free to create your own letter variations also—just remember to keep your slant consistent.

UPPERCASE UPBEAT SCRIPT

After you trace the letter examples for the lowercase, try the uppercase alphabet, then experiment further on your own paper with letter joins. Because this style is more casual, each letter in a word does not need to be connected. This allows the text to look more individualistic and edgy instead of perfectly refined.

●◆ Unattached versus Attached Flourish

Taking your time is one of the most crucial tips for hand lettering. Practice executing the unattached flourish at the bottom of the design to match the top attached flourish.

abcdefghijklm

nopqrstuvwxyz

keep it simple

ABCDEFGHIJKLM

NOPQRSTUVWXYZ

Seize the Day!

Playful Script

Playful Script is a variation that looks attractive and is super useful in designs. Because the ascenders and descenders are fairly short and loops are relatively small, this script is compact, legible, and ideal for designs where you want to conserve space. With its round shapes and smooth, unobtrusive appearance, it also pairs well with other styles of writing. The carefree capitals give this script a whimsical look, and the letters are connected in even, tidy rows that work well for longer texts. You can make these letters slightly italicized, like the following examples, or you can experiment with making them more vertical for a somewhat different look. You can even write Playful Script with left-leaning letters if you'd like!

LOWERCASE PLAYFUL SCRIPT

Trace these lowercase letters in groups of six or seven to get the flow of the letter joins, then write the words "find balance" in your practice notebook.

UPPERCASE PLAYFUL SCRIPT

Now you're ready to move on to the capital letters! Practice these in the space below each example. Then, for extra enjoyment, try putting the lowercase and uppercase together by writing out your favorite song lyrics or addressing an envelope using the Playful Script style.

●◆ Keep Your Slant Consistent

Noticing beauty will help you implement new ideas into your work. Practice keeping a consistent slant and smooth flourishes by tracing these words here, then repeating them in your practice notebook.

abcdefg hijklmn

opqrstu vwxyz

find balance

A B C D E F G H I

J K L M N O P Q

R S T U V W X Y Z

Fancy Capitals

When a word demands extra attention, these Fancy Capitals are perfect to have in your repertoire! You can see how they have some extra loops or twirls at the beginning of the entrance stroke or somewhere else in the letter.

While Fancy Capitals definitely showcase extravagance, they can also serve a practical purpose. When you want to extend a word on a line, a Fancy Capital may be just what you need to take up more space, express the meaning of the text through flourishing, or bring balance to a design.

Keep in mind that there are endless variations for script capitals; you'll see other examples of flourished capitals in the project pages in Part 2. Some will resonate with you more than others, so it's helpful to keep a little alphabetized notebook to record your favorites and draw from when you need inspiration. In the meantime, try tracing these and scripting your own on practice paper.

Print Styles to Match Word Meanings

Print styles provide the perfect contrast to script when you are developing designs. They can be used for emphasis, swift readability, or to break up a longer text. Having versatile print styles to choose from will be an essential part of almost any design. When selecting a style, pause to consider the mood of what you are portraying and choose a style that best fits that meaning. Think of the styles that you will master in this book as part of an ever-expanding library that you can add to regularly.

Printed alphabets can be written with a variety of pens, pencils, brushes, and inks. You'll want to make these decisions depending on the size, weight, and style you need for your design.

✏ Practice Joyful Letters

It's essential to tune out distractions and be present so you can get in the creative flow as you hand letter! Try to create an airy, joyful vibe while penning these flourishes.

Empowered Print

Use the Empowered Print alphabet when crisply legible letters are required for a design. Trace these letters while you focus on writing clean, straight lines and keeping an even slant. The curves are subtle, making the letters a bit more rectangular.

LOWERCASE EMPOWERED PRINT
You can practice this alphabet using a monoline pen or a brush pen if you'd like to add weight to the downstrokes.

UPPERCASE EMPOWERED PRINT
For extra practice to check your spacing, grab your notebook or a piece of lined/ graph paper and try the capitals. Then write out anything that comes to mind: a grocery or to-do list, months of the year, names of your best friends, or the song lyrics you're listening to. When you're done, check your page to see if your spacing is even, if your slants remain at the same angle throughout your page, and if all your letters are about the same height and width. Turn your page upside down to focus on the letters as shapes. This way, you'll be able to spot any holes, crowdedness, or letters that are demanding unwanted attention.

Confident Print

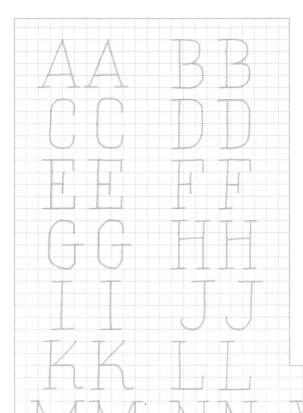

This variation is similar to the Empowered Print alphabet you just practiced, but it has serifs, those little lines added to the ends of letter strokes. (Letters without these additions are called sans serif.) Place the serifs on the tops and bottoms as you write each stroke, or you may find it's easiest to add serifs after completely writing the letter or even after writing all your text. Whatever method you choose, just make sure to give your letters a little breathing room so there's enough space to add the serifs.

Serif alphabets tend to look more distinct and sophisticated, so they have great potential to add strength and significance to your designs. They complement other lettering styles well, so they will come in handy for multi-style designs. Depending on the spacing of your text, there's room for variation: Serifs can be small or more pronounced. It is important to make sure they are all about the same size so the overall appearance of your design looks cohesive. If you like, you can add weight to the downstrokes for a bolder look, as is shown in the word *strong* on the previous page. Trace those letters and the word *strong*, and, for additional practice, write similar words in your notebook that "fit" this lettering style!

Uppercase Simply Timeless Print

This is a great go-to style for lettering within banners when you want a straightforward, easy-to-read option. This Simply Timeless alphabet is monoline, meaning the weight of the lines is the same throughout (no thicks or thins). If you plan to use larger letters in this style, you can either use a thicker monoline pen or a straight-edged or brush pen to vary the up-and-down strokes just like you learned to do for script.

This simple sans serif uppercase alphabet is extremely adaptable. If you want to change it up, add serifs. You can also slant the letters to show forward movement or contrast in a design that already has vertical letters. You can make the letters taller, shorter, wider, or narrower—each of these changes will give your alphabet an entirely new feel. There are also opportunities for creativity within the letters; you can vary the way you write the cross bars on the *A* and *H* by crossing them extra high or extra low. Just slight differences give the letters more personality. The "leg" of the *K* and *R* is another prime example: It can extend out dramatically, end in a flourish, or kick up to show emotion.

Here, you can trace the entire Simply Timeless alphabet. For further practice, copy the alphabet in your notebook.

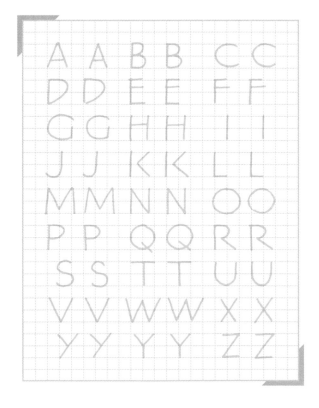

Lowercase Vintage Type Print

To write lowercase letters with serifs, try this Vintage Type Print. Reminiscent of old-fashioned typewriter print, this style has an enduring appeal. Vintage Type Print is great to use when you have a longer quote, and it pairs nicely with both script and print styles. Even though type print may seem familiar, when hand lettered, it has an endearing and authentically human quality that can work well in many of your designs.

Like all the alphabets, Vintage Type Print gives you a chance to slow down when writing letters and concentrate on elements such as good spacing, even pressure, and similar-sized serifs. Notice the little scoops at the ends of the letters *a*, *d*, *h*, *i*, *l*, *m*, and so on. When practicing, focus on making them smooth and rounded and as close as possible to the same size throughout your page. If you prefer serifs to scoops, feel free to replace them by writing a straight line and placing a serif at the end of the stroke; you can try a few variations at the end of the alphabet.

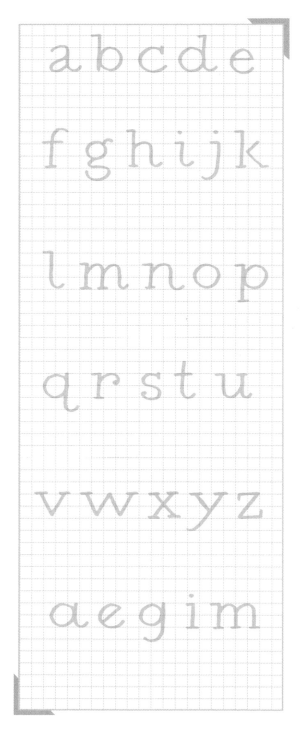

Whimsy Print --

Carefree and lighthearted, Whimsy Print will bring a mindful lift to your designs. Even though it follows some general guidelines, this alphabet is not as picky about writing completely straight lines and maintaining a perfectly uniform size and slant. In fact, the attraction of these letters is their subtle imperfections. When you'd like to express a mood that is childlike, whimsical, or informal, try incorporating this alphabet into your design. It's a versatile alphabet that is also perfect to use in functional ways—such as a quick greeting card or gift tag. This style also works well for menus, signs, posters, chalkboards, and bullet journaling!

    This sample is in lightweight monoline, but you can experiment in your notebook with different-sized bullet tips. You may also enjoy writing this style with a brush pen, colorful gel pens, or a paintbrush and watercolors. Trace these uppercase and lowercase letters, and then create your own in the blank space beneath each letter.

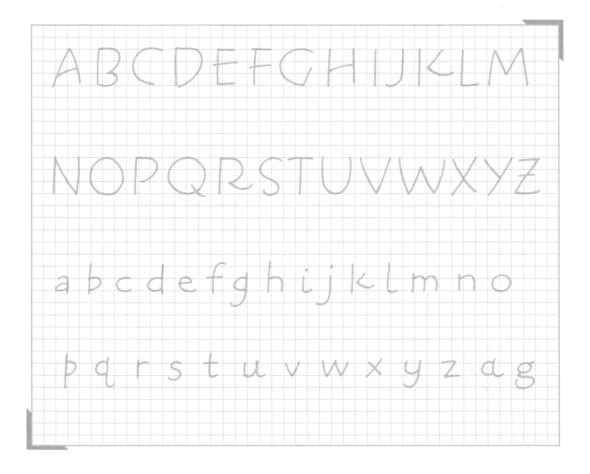

Uppercase Festive Print

This Festive Print alphabet, made with double lines, is another way to dress up a basic alphabet. It's really fun to use, and you can add your own creative touches too. Write the letter first, then add one parallel line (for the round letters, draw a straight line inside the arc). After tracing the examples, use the space below the letters to re-create your own. You can also practice writing words in your notebook. Spacing can be a little tricky to get used to—remember to leave enough room between letters to accommodate the double line.

Simple Versals

Simple Versals is a style that offers a unique freedom for play and creativity. One of the best things about this alphabet is the way the letters relate to each other, sometimes even joining in eccentric ligatures (which you can watch for in Part 2 of this book). For example, two *L*'s can nestle together, or the second line in your *H* can become the backbone for the *E* that follows. If you can ensure easy readability, all kinds of inventive ideas are possible with this alphabet! Trace the sample alphabet, then play around with creating your alphabet in the practice space.

Decorative Styles

The following styles are a little different from the previous print and script alphabets you've been working on. They are drawn with double sides, so it takes a little more time and effort to get the parallel lines straight and consistent for all the letters in your word or phrase. But the practice they require is well worth it! These alphabets have unique options—they can be left open or filled in countless different ways. You can fill them in completely with black ink or with colors, or you can fill them with patterns. You can leave them partially open and fill in just the top or bottom section. Depending on your design, you can also adjust these alphabets in size, thickness, slant, and shading—however you think they look best!

●◆ Review Your Progress

Every once in a while, briefly survey your older practice pages and note what you're proud of and where you'd like to improve. While writing this, aim for consistent slant and spacing.

Statement Letters

This versatile hand-drawn alphabet is ideal when you want a word to clearly stand out. You can leave Statement Letters open or fill them in. You can also customize this alphabet easily by varying the height, width, slant, and spacing of the letters. To further highlight letters, draw a shadow to the right of each one. The thickness of the shade depends on your design: Use a thin shade when trying to conserve space on the line or try a thick shade to fill up extra space. Whatever shade size you choose, try to keep it consistent throughout your piece. This particular alphabet shade is super easy since it doesn't extend below or above the letters but only follows the contour of the letter directly to the right.

Trace the letters first, then trace the shade. You can use a gray shading marker, a regular pencil, or a gray-colored pencil. When you use Statement Letters for your projects, you can also shade with other colors or use a mono-line pen to fill the shaded area with diagonal lines or cross-hatching. Your options are limitless!

For another variation, filling in the counters of letters is a lighthearted way of bringing extra charisma to a design. Trace these letters with filled-in counters. For more practice, in your notebook, write a word or name that contains some letters with counters or make a thank-you card or bullet journal spread using this alphabet.

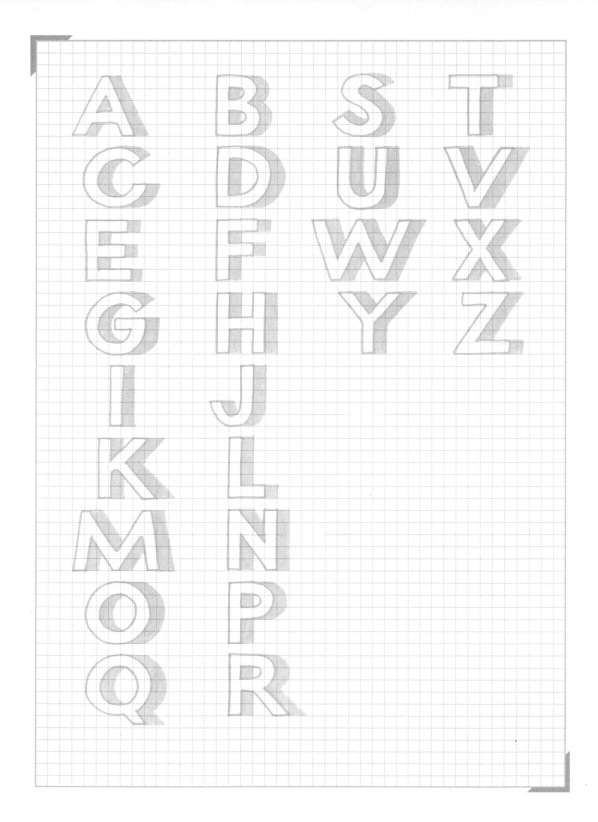

Bold Alphabet

When you adjust the thicknesses of these letters, they take on a different personality. Take a minute to compare the Statement Letters with this Bold Alphabet style and notice the thick and thin letter segments before tracing the letters. For extra practice, write your name and phone number in this style.

Resilience Alphabet

Now you're ready to add serifs to a fill-in alphabet style! For this Resilience Alphabet, you'll use thin and thick segments for the letters and cap them with narrow, rectangular serifs to add more personality. Get familiar with where the letters are thickest (downstrokes and middle section of rounded letters like *O* and *C*). The *A*, *N*, and *M* start with an upstroke, which is why the first part of those letters is narrow instead of having the customary wide downstroke of letters like the *B* and *E*. Trace these letters here, and for further practice, try writing a few words in your separate notebook.

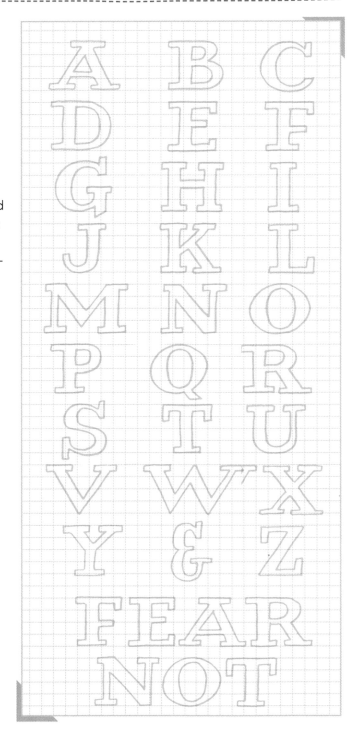

Jubilant Alphabet

Sometimes you will want weighty, hand-drawn letters that are italicized, and this alphabet will fill that need. You'll notice that some of the letters have decorative round terminals—another example of how to add distinction to an alphabet. However, sometimes leaving them off will fit better for a certain design, so remember that all the terminal endings can finish in a hairline curve as well. Trace these examples, and for further practice, draw the alphabet in your separate notebook.

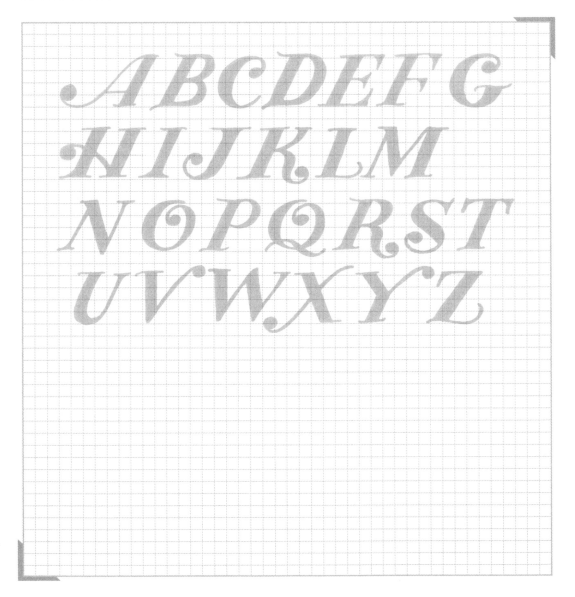

Romantic Script

Fill-in script letters can be a little high-maintenance! Figuring out letter joins, spacing, and how to handle counters, while keeping everything legible, is a tall order, but it's fun to try after you've had a little practice with the print options. Here's a little taste via Romantic Script for you to trace and then copy in the blank space underneath the word. If you want an extra challenge, try writing a few more words in your separate notebook to test your lettering prowess. You can leave them open, as this example illustrates, or fill in the letters with black or other colors if desired.

Elements of Design

Now that you have a library of versatile alphabets to choose from, it's time to move on to learning some basic design principles. Even though these guidelines are simple to understand and execute, they will revolutionize your work! Follow these step-by-step instructions and remember to start small. Consistently applying these principles will result in rapid improvement in taking your designs to the next level.

Seven Steps for Quote Designs

1. **Write out the quote in your regular handwriting on grid or lined practice paper.** Now you know what you are working with.

2. **Underline and circle key words as you think about the meaning and importance of each word.** Look for repeated words, important themes, and words or phrases you want to emphasize. Sometimes it's strategic to put dividers at the natural breaks in the quote or helpful to take a word or letter count. I like to read the quote aloud at least once. One artist I know always acts out the text of the piece with movements to help physically feel the meaning of the quote before he chooses how to display it on paper. It may seem silly, but these little exercises can help enormously in creating a pleasing final piece.

3. **Begin to doodle the quote using whatever styles you feel like.** This is a time to play, so don't worry about precision or perfection, just start fitting the words together with freedom and no concern about "making a mistake." Refer to the styles in this book for ideas, along with any other alphabets that you've collected for inspiration. If something doesn't seem to be working, feel free to abandon the page and give yourself a fresh blank page to start again. Allow one idea to lead to another. Use contrast to create interest. Sometimes the quote will begin to take a literal shape like an oval or a rectangle due to the length and spacing of the words and how you are choosing to highlight certain words.

4. **Write the passage as many times as necessary until you arrive at the layout and lettering that click for you.** When you settle on a design, it often helps to write another rough draft to clean up any sloppy areas and give your brain a little more time to examine all the decisions you've made and assess for any possible improvements.

5. **Analyze for legibility, balance, cleanness of design (not too busy), sizing and spacing of words, and overall appeal of the piece.** Check flourishes,

embellishments, and illustrations to ensure they add to the piece and pull the design together rather than detract from the text and meaning.

6. **Show someone else!** Ask for feedback, especially to see if there are any challenges with legibility or following the layout of the quote. If no one's around to voice an opinion, take a picture and review that yourself. It's astonishing how often a photo will reveal what needs tweaking—things that weren't obvious while looking at the actual paper. Stepping away from your design overnight and coming back to it in the morning with fresh eyes is also extremely helpful.

7. **Make any adjustments, then re-create your piece on fine paper or bright white smooth paper if you plan to digitize your design.** Use a ruler or guidelines for the best possible spacing and to keep your letter sizes uniform. After the design is penciled in, use the desired pens, ink, watercolor, gouache, or whatever you've selected to complete your piece. Be sure to let any ink or paint thoroughly dry before erasing any pencil marks. The more you repeat this process, the more you will see your own unique talents, preferences, and styles emerging!

Troubleshooting

Sometimes when you are excited about a design, it's easy to ignore some of its drawbacks. While a design may "work," there might be another way of developing it that is more readable, consistent, balanced, and attractive. To learn how to troubleshoot potential issues, let's look at the same quote done two different ways to point out common mistakes and how to take a design from mediocre to magnificent!

⬤◆ Personalize Your Exercises

Whenever you come across a difficult spot in a letter, take a second to single out that stroke and add it to your page of warm-up exercises. This way, you can personalize warm-up exercises to fit your needs. Besides seeing results more quickly, you'll also feel more relaxed and at ease with letters that challenge you.

The First Version

Legibility is one of the most important aspects of design. If either the letters themselves or the order of the lettering is confusing, the reader will struggle to quickly read and grasp the meaning. Your goal is for the reader to easily decipher the words and for all illustrations and flourishing to support the text, not distract from it. In this design, there are obvious areas of confusion:

- "You're braver than you believe" is written in a maze that is hard to follow.

- The descender of the first *Y* swoops around to make the top of the printed *T* for the vertical *THAN* and is not an easy transition to read.

- The flourishes in the entrance stroke of the first *You* are a little too large and pronounced for the size of the word.

- Using the tail of the *Y* to cross the *T* in *THAN* may "work," but it's preferable to avoid unnatural-looking stretches where it looks like the flourish is working extra hard to perform an athletic feat.

- The word *THINK* at the end of the quote is top-heavy with flourishes that don't serve a clear purpose.

- The top of the *T* in *THINK* as part of a flourish and the forced turn into the downstroke of the *H* make the word less readable than it could be.

Consistency cannot be overstressed when creating designs. Take a minute to jot down the interpretation issues and areas of inconsistency in this example before reading this list. Here are the major ones:

- **The word *Braver*:** This word uses all lowercase, except for one capital letter.

- **The word *Believe*:** The first four letters sit on the base line and are similar in size, and the last three letters bounce up and down and change sizes.

- **The word *Stronger*:** The letters show an inconsistency in style as well as size: Mid-word, they switch from print capitals to lowercase script.

- **The words *Than You*:** These words in the banner show an inconsistency in slant and weight. The *Than You* at the bottom of the quote also demonstrates an inconsistency in slant, with some letters italicized and some upright.

- **The large *AND*:** The stems of the letters in *AND* are not at a consistent slant. Also, you can see a common error in the *A* and *N* since these letters are very easy to write improperly. For an *A*, the first stroke should be a thin upstroke, and the second, a thick downstroke. Similarly for an *N*, the first stroke should be a thin upstroke, the middle diagonal stroke is thick, and the third vertical stroke is a thin upstroke (the *N* in *THINK* shows another example of this).

- **Lack of proper word emphasis:** Identify the important words and position them as the lead actors onstage. In this design, the short word

AND is written in a bolder and bigger style than the other words (as well as the last *Than You*), and key words like *braver*, *stronger*, and *smarter* aren't given the center stage they deserve. Although this design displays a lot of different lettering styles, it's clear that this was written without giving thought to the meanings of the words and how to best represent them with intentional design.

- **Inconsistent flourishing:** With flourishing, it's often more attractive to use similar flourishing elements throughout a design. Here, the flourishes are too varied in style and are moving in multiple directions. Another thing to consider is keeping flourishes on the outside of the design when possible. There may be exceptions to the rule, but not having a lot of bulky flourishing trapped within the design generally improves balance, flow, and legibility.

- **Use of symbol versus text:** The plus symbol (+) is generally okay to use, but here, before the word *stronger*, it's a little crowded and hard to decipher. Plus signs and ampersands can enhance designs when used thoughtfully, but it always pays off to take a few minutes to determine if writing out the word is preferable.

- **Busyness:** Another consideration is the busyness of your design. There can be a place for multiple styles and a busy vibe, but avoid an overloaded smorgasbord of lettering styles and images. Here, you can see a conglomeration of styles that don't really complement each other or provide a pleasant contrast, but instead seem to be competing for attention. For example, on the first line (*You're braver*), you can see how two super-similar styles next to each other usually don't look as good as two contrasting styles.

- **Lack of illustration cohesiveness:** This design also lacks intentional repetition, which lends strength and appeal to your text. Using repetitive elements of a certain flourish or illustration makes a stronger impact than squeezing a ton of different ones into one design. Here, the illustrations are so varied that it's difficult to attribute any meaning to them. This design includes a sprig of leaves, wavy lines, a heart, a flower, an arrow, a star, water drops, and a sun; it's difficult to figure out how each illustration is symbolizing the text.

- **Lack of text centering or alignment:** Centering text is an important skill for creating designs. Here, no attempt is made to center; instead, illustrations are used to fill in any empty white space. Typically, that's a great strategy, but too much of this technique can cause a design to feel lopsided. Much of this quote could benefit from some simple centering, and even centering the attribution line would be an easy fix.

- **Unclear punctuation:** Punctuation marks should look natural and not draw attention to themselves. Because the word *Seem* is written at a slant and followed by a comma, the punctuation mark looks like it's floating in the air next to the word *and* that follows. It could be mistaken for an apostrophe and bewilder the reader. Because you know exactly what you're writing and are spending a lot of time on an intricate design, it will always be understandable to you. But someone reading it for the first time may encounter some hindrances to legibility that you haven't considered. This is where another pair of eyes can be very helpful. Whenever possible, show your work to someone who doesn't know what you're writing and gauge their ability to read it effortlessly to gain whatever valuable feedback they can offer.

The Revised Version

Now let's look at the second design, using the same quote. You can see how this one has a clean look that is easy to follow. There are only three lettering styles used, a combination of both script and print styles. Notice how the styles complement one another and provide interesting contrast by using different slants and thicknesses.

The three key words that I wanted to stress in the quote—*braver*, *stronger*, and *smarter*—stand out by being tall, italicized, and monoline, in contrast to the thicker brush script and upright capitals.

The flourishes within the design are subtle and don't overtake the words; there are just a few scarf-like swashes off the brush letters that allude to movement for visual interest. The larger flourishing on the top and bottom gives a finishing touch that ties the design together. The flourishes aren't identical, but you can see how they look related. They are similar in size, shape, and style, which brings a cohesive feel to the design.

Another thing to note that wasn't evident in the first, busier design is the repetition of the three repeated *than you* phrases. These are treated exactly the same here, written small and clearly so they are easy to read, but not attracting too much attention since they are supporting words. The line of dots is for the benefit of the reader's eye, lengthening the line to make it more like the rest of the lines in the piece.

Centering is also used throughout the design, including the attribution line at the bottom.

As far as illustrations, you can see there's a vast difference between the two designs. For this one, I chose a simple illustration that I use often because it is fitting for most designs: a star composed of straight lines. It is a charming way to fill in a few empty spots and add a little burst of visual interest that accents the meaning of the text. In designs, you can also take advantage of subtle opportunities, like how you dot the *i*'s, to add a touch of hand lettered whimsy. Here, I dotted the two *i*'s with two tiny circles.

Creative Entrance Strokes

Now that you have a broad understanding of design principles and some great troubleshooting abilities, let's zoom in on another fun skill to practice to amp up your designs even more: capital letter entrance strokes.

Here are ten different entrance strokes that can be modified for many of the script capital letter styles and that will add a lot of finesse to your designs. First, trace the entrance strokes alone using a brush pen, then re-create your own before using them to form letters. After finishing this page, spend as much time with these variations in your separate practice notebook as you like.

I like to use these ten embellished entrance strokes primarily with the letters H, K, M, N, U, V, W, X, Y, and Z. Some of the variations also work well for the second stroke of B, P, R, T, and F.

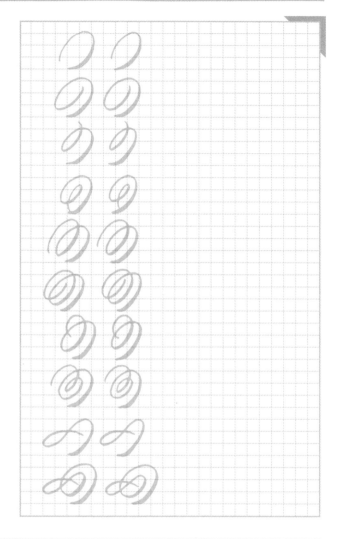

Using Entrance Strokes in Words

Now let's put those entrance strokes to work! *Happy Birthday* is a phrase you can use in everyday projects, so here are some examples to get started. After tracing and writing these, you can use some of the other ten entrance strokes for additional practice. Conveniently, you can also apply these entrance strokes to *Happy New Year*! Again, trace and re-create these, then feel free to experiment with your own variations in your separate notebook, referring back to the entrance strokes as needed.

Flourishing Progression Activity

One fun way to explore different flourishing opportunities is through this progression exercise. You can use any word as well as any script or print style. Start as simple as possible and challenge yourself to slowly build more intricate designs as you create. Because you're working with only one word, it's less intimidating than designing an entire quote. There's no pressure involved, and you have the freedom to go out on a limb and try anything. While you are worry-free and just having fun creating, you may surprise yourself with new combinations of flourishes you'd never considered before! Even though many designs won't make the final cut, they still contribute to your learning process and proficiency. Trace these sample progressions (*Congrats* in script, and *Enjoy* in print), then choose a couple of words to do on your own. When you discover a progression that leads to a balanced and attractive outcome, give it a star, and try to come up with a handful that you can showcase in your practice notebook.

➻ Be Observant

Look around for gorgeous letters! As you go about your day, try to spot unique signs, posters, book covers, and other items for hand lettering inspiration. While writing "Look Around," leave the last stroke of the letter off the *k* and *d* and come back at the end to connect the two letters.

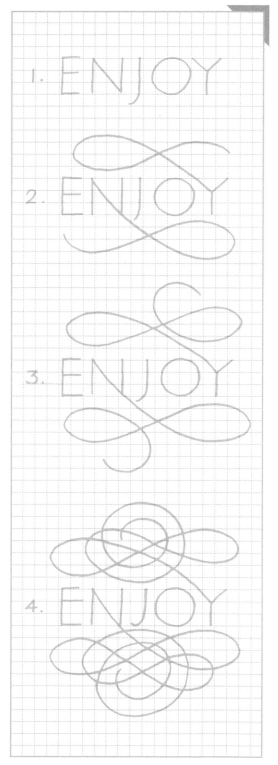

Building Block Activities

Before you design entire lettering projects, it's a great idea to get some practice with short two- or three-word phrases to get the hang of making simpler design decisions. Then you're more prepared for the lengthier projects coming up in Part 2! Now that you have practiced your lettering, shading, flourishing, and other elements, try designing a few of your own favorite extra-short phrases. Here are four script and four print mini projects to re-create in the space below each phrase, or in your separate notebook if you need more room, that will allow you to use many of the alphabets that you've already practiced!

●◆ Practice Downstrokes and Upstrokes

The sheer thrill of creating shows in your work, so make time for play! While writing this, focus on beautiful swells in your downstrokes and delicate upstrokes.

Script Projects

These four options will give you lots to work with:

1. Write "You Matter" and try your hand at an unattached flourish. These are ideal when you don't have descender letters to work off of.
2. Write "Hey, Beautiful" using the entrance strokes you learned earlier and practice some fun flourishing to underline the design.
3. Write "Yes, you can" both ways. Which do you like the best?
4. Now try "Do what you love" two different ways in your notebook using the modern Upbeat Script and a heavily flourished Copperplate. Which one is your favorite?

Print Projects

These four activities focus primarily on print styles, but you will also get a taste of mixing script with print as a design technique.

1. Using Festive Print with some Spencerian lowercase for contrast, write "Practice makes Progress" in the blank space provided.
2. Write the outline for "All In" in Bold Alphabet style, and for a skill-building exercise, neatly fill in around it in ink to make the letters pop.
3. Now for some shading practice! Write "Try" and "New" in italicized Statement Letters and add shading. Then write "something" in Spencerian lowercase.
4. Then write "Consistency is Key," which will give you practice in both shading and combining three styles: Empowered Print and Bold Alphabet, with a small dose of Spencerian script in the banner.

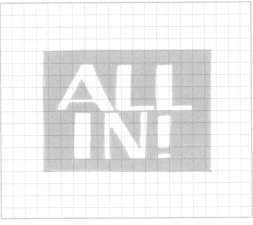

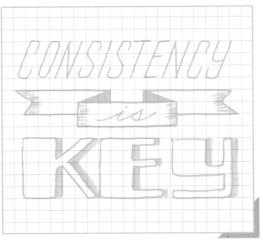

Purposeful Projects

*"Art is unquestionably one of the purest and highest elements
in human happiness."*

—John Lubbock

Part 2 packs in fifty unique and exciting projects to take you on a journey of applying your skills to the positive quotes and affirmations that make up each activity. You will learn how to use multiple lettering styles; incorporate banners, flourishes, and illustrations; and find creative ways to express the meaning of the text through the elements and styles you select. The projects will increase in difficulty, so you get a chance to gradually build upon your skills through the helpful instructional pages on the left-hand side of each two-page spread. As you move through the projects, you'll find that the encouraging words you write will do more than build your lettering competence; they will lift your spirit as well!

As you dive into Part 2, there are three main areas where you can test your observation skills and establish good habits to apply to your designs. First, decide which key words to emphasize. Each design is just one interpretation—you might choose a different emphasis to show how a particular quote speaks most powerfully to you. Second, choose a style of writing. In each design, count how many different styles of writing are used. You will see a wide range (from one style to eight styles used in a single design, like in the Create a Multi-Style Design project), and as you observe, think about how these design decisions represent the meanings of the words. Third, consider any contrasting styles. Here are some examples: script and print, slanted and upright, serif and sans serif, large and small, thick and thin, shaded and unshaded, ornate and plain, all caps and lowercase. When you create your own designs, you can also use color for additional visual contrast. Enjoy the journey!

Lengthen Short Lines of Text

When you're designing quotes, you may end up with lines that have only a couple of short words. To even out the text vertically, you may want to extend those words so they take up more space. One way of lengthening shorter lines when they are in script is to exaggerate an entrance or exit stroke. It's fun to practice, and it looks graceful and elegant in designs.

For this design, the challenge was how to keep the small supporting phrases *I am* and *in my* from disappearing into the background. For aesthetics, I wanted a layout that roughly formed a block shape to show security and stability, the theme of the quote.

You can elongate these letters either at the end or beginning of the line. I alternated the extensions on the left and right for balance: *I am* extends at the end of the line, and *in my*, at the beginning. Elongating strokes also works great when you are scripting shorter names and need them to fill more space.

Try it: Practice elongating some lowercase letters so you can work this skill into your designs when needed. Trace these examples, then create your own in the blank practice box.

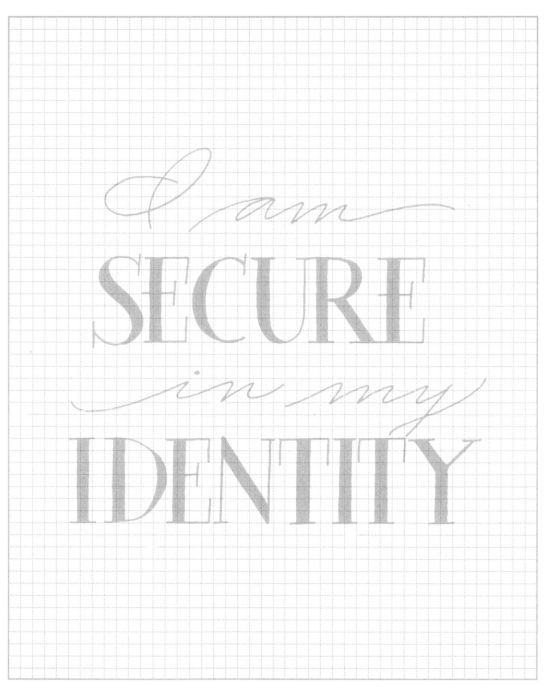

I am SECURE *in my* IDENTITY

NOW IT'S YOUR TURN!

Trace this design here, then re-create it in your own way on a piece of paper or in a frame at the back of this book.

Create Twin Flourishes Using Ascenders and Descenders

Twin flourishes work the most naturally when words contain ascenders and descenders. Be on the lookout for these flourishing opportunities, and have fun adding them to your layouts! The flourishes in this quote were designed to be large and generous, like a warm hug, to fit with the message of the text: being kind to yourself. Since the quote is short, only one lettering style is used, with the embellishment providing the contrast and appeal to the design.

Remember to keep flourishes oval-shaped and practice keeping the lines smooth. You can shade them with your brush pen if you like, just as you would shade letters, or you can keep them light without shading by not applying any pressure with your brush. Another option is to switch to a monoline pen for the flourishing portions.

Try it: Trace the three steps in the examples, following the arrows. Then create your own ascender and descender flourishes in the blank practice box.

1.

2.

3.

4.

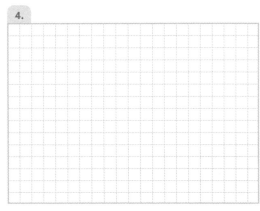

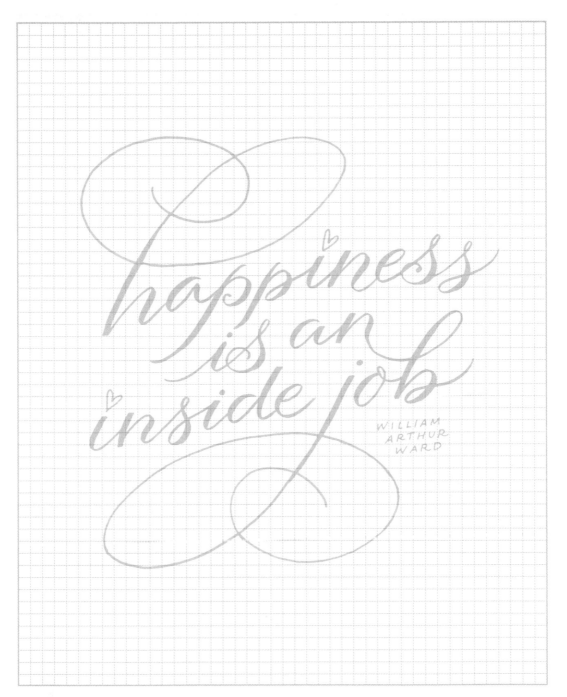

happiness is an inside job

WILLIAM
ARTHUR
WARD

Trace this design here, then re-create it in your own way on a piece
of paper or in a frame at the back of this book.

Use Compass Points to Symbolize Meaning

When you are looking for a subtle way to express meaning, these compass points are a great element to keep in mind. In this quote, you can see how all four cardinal directions are represented simply by extending one letter stroke on each line, which helps to demonstrate the meaning of the word *more*. You can make the extended lines thin or thick; here, I thickened the ends of the lines to balance the weight of the bold letters in *MORE*.

When it fits with your text, this skill is an easy and attractive way to add some strength, interest, and creativity to your design. When you add the extensions to your letter strokes, it's a great idea to have someone look at the text to make certain it is easy to read.

Try it: Trace these letters and their horizontal and vertical extensions, then rewrite them in the space provided. Then use the blank box to practice writing the word *MORE*, focusing on keeping the same thickness for each letter.

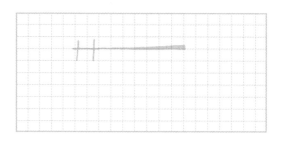

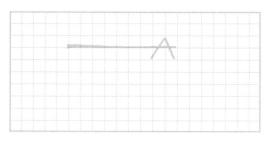

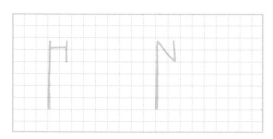

NOW IT'S YOUR TURN!

Trace this design here, then re-create it in your own way on a piece of paper or in a frame at the back of this book.

Be Creative with Double Letters

When you come across double letters, pause and think about how you want to treat them in your design. They are a great opportunity for creativity! Ask yourself if it's advantageous to keep them identical, or would it work well to give them subtle or obvious differences? Double letters are a hand letterer's dream because you get to choose!

Because there are two sets of doubles here, you can try a couple of methods. You can challenge yourself to make the two hand-drawn *P*'s as identical as possible, and then, for the script double *p*'s, give the first one a flamboyant flourish. You can also flourish both *p*'s if you prefer; just remember to keep your lines parallel.

A couple more tips: Use stars or simple, repetitive illustrations to fill in blank spots in your design. And remember, you don't always have to stay on the line! Did you know that writing on a slightly upward slope shows optimism? Here, you can see that *think* and *be happy* are on a slight upward slant.

Try it: Let's practice some doubles! Trace the *P*'s here and give the double flourish a try. Exercise your own creative expression with double letters in the blank practice box.

Trace this design here, then re-create it in your own way on a piece of paper or in a frame at the back of this book.

Try the Resilience Alphabet

This alphabet (introduced on page 39) is an ideal choice for a word or phrase you want to emphasize. Here, the theme of this affirmation is the word *enough*, and you can see how this style highlights the word and meaning. The illustrations serve to lengthen the lines where the text isn't long enough to match the larger writing. For balance, you can alternate the leaves on either side of the text.

Try it: Letters with serifs always require a little more practice. Take your time and concentrate on getting the thick and thin parts of the letters correct. While the serifs don't have to be perfect, you want them to all be approximately the same size and thickness. First, practice drawing all the lines needed to create the serif, as shown in the left-hand boxes, then erase your pencil lines after inking. Use the right-hand boxes to practice writing the letters freehand without the extra serif lines.

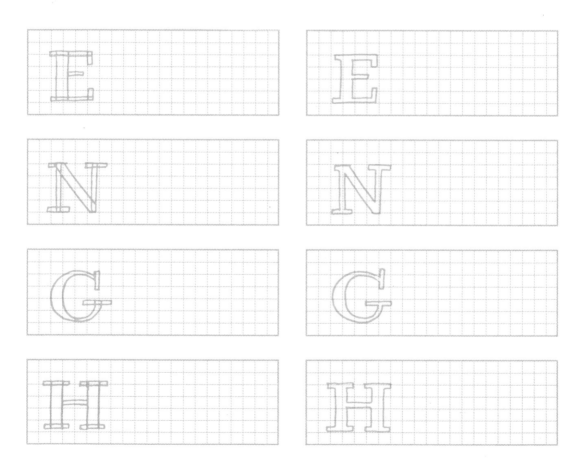

Trace this design here, then re-create it in your own way on a piece of paper or in a frame at the back of this book.

Incorporate Statement Letters Into a Design

Statement Letters (see page 37 for the entire alphabet) are a great choice for words you want to emphasize within a quote. You can make them large or small, short or tall, shaded or filled in. They are easy to read and pair well with other styles of writing.

In this example, the letters are shaded to add dimension, and the capital *O* of the Statement Letter alphabet provides a perfect circle for both an ascender and descender to wrap around. These kinds of tweaks are fun to explore, especially when they make the meaning of your text come to life. Use your imagination to create letters with personality, incorporating strokes that show movement, exuberance, and relationships with one another. The *t*-crossing here turns into a dramatic underline flourish with a joyful loop at the end, giving the design a little extra charisma.

Try it: Trace these three steps of the *F* to get familiar with Statement Letters before writing them on your own in the blank space next to the letter. Then put it all together with the letter *Y* in the last practice box.

1.

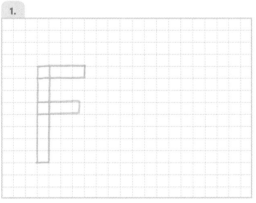

2.

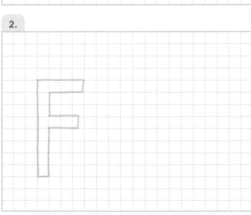

3.

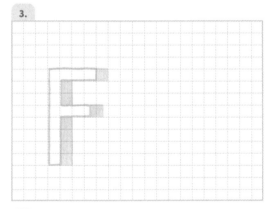

4.

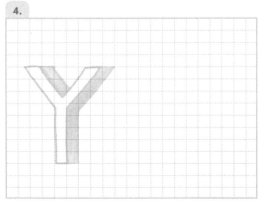

FIND
what brings
you
JOY
and go
there

JAN
PHILLIPS

Trace this design here, then re-create it in your own way on a piece of paper or in a frame at the back of this book.

Festive Print (see the full alphabet on page 33) is a versatile style to use in your layouts. You can easily add serifs to the double lines, or you can leave the letters open or filled with stripes, dots, or other patterns. In this final quote, the letters are half-filled with diagonal lines.

Try it: Here is a sampling of different letter fillings in the word *beautiful*, written in sans serif Festive Print. Copy the patterns in the unfilled letters, then rewrite the word in the blank area below the words. Enjoy coming up with some of your own creative patterns. You can fill in the letters completely, halfway, or in any combination you wish.

I am UNIQUELY positioned to make a POSITIVE difference in the world!

NOW IT'S YOUR TURN!

Trace this design here, then re-create it in your own way on a piece of paper or in a frame at the back of this book.

Create a Copperplate Script–Based Design

Copperplate is a classic and popular style that is versatile for many of your designs. (To refer back to the whole alphabet, see pages 17 and 19.) In this exercise, the quote fits loosely into a square shape. Just one style, a Copperplate variation, is used, but the flourishing and leaf illustrations off of the word *happiness* highlight the word and express the meaning of the quote. Keeping everything else fairly simple gives the piece an orderly yet elegant look.

Try it: With a medium-sized brush pen, trace the words and then rewrite them in the blank practice boxes. Focus on consistent slant and spacing as well as achieving smooth letter joins. After you feel comfortable with these words, try writing *happiness* in your practice notebook with flourishing on both ends!

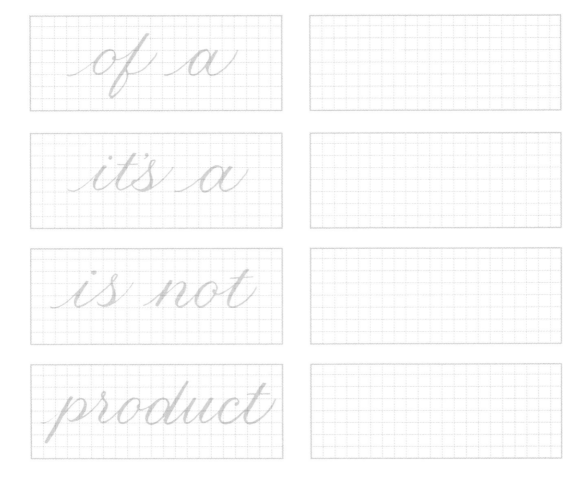

Trace this design here, then re-create it in your own way on a piece of paper or in a frame at the back of this book.

Strategically Place Illustrations for Balance and Meaning

Sometimes an off-center illustration is exactly what a design needs. When you have an otherwise balanced design, keep an eye open for spaces to slip in an illustration on just one side of a shorter line of text.

This present moment was a natural theme to highlight, and the phrase is conveniently centered in the text. But the short word *this* left about half the line blank! Rather than center it and try to fill two holes, I liked the effect of positioning an asymmetrical illustration to the right of the word. The bold sun gives the design balance and heightens the significance of living in the now.

Try it: Trace the outline of the letters, then fill them in however you'd like. Feel free to use colors, sparkle pens, and any patterns you like. Then draw the sun or another illustration that you think represents finding happiness in this moment.

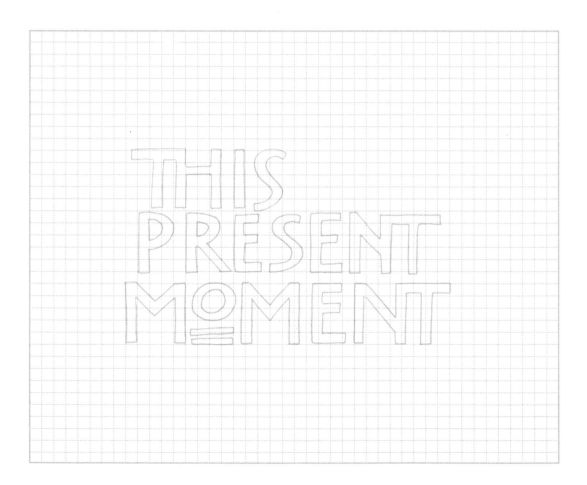

I am capable of living in THIS PRESENT MOMENT and finding happiness here

Trace this design here, then re-create it in your own way on a piece of paper or in a frame at the back of this book.

Set an Informal Tone with Upbeat Script

Upbeat Script (see the full alphabet on page 23) works great when you want an informal vibe. This script was an ideal contrast to the simple capitals in the game pieces. Centering the Upbeat Script above and below the key word *happy* helps with easy readability and a neat appearance.

Using a brush pen gives some weight to the letters, but you can also use a monoline tool if that looks better with your design. In Upbeat Script, letter joins are less formal, and you can also make your letters "bounce" a little by not starting every single letter exactly on the line.

Try it: Write some words before you practice using Upbeat Script in a design. First, trace the word, then rewrite it in the space provided, keeping a consistent slant, thick downstrokes, and delicate upstrokes. When you're finished, you can also evaluate your spacing between letters—does it look even?

Most folks,
are usually
about as
H A P P Y
as they make
up their
minds to be

• A B R A H A M   L I N C O L N •

NOW IT'S YOUR TURN!

Trace this design here, then re-create it in your own way on a piece of paper or in a frame at the back of this book.

Highlight a Word with Balanced Flourishing

If your focus word has easy-to-flourish letters, balanced flourishing is a useful skill to keep in mind. Remember to try a lot of different options until you find something that you like!

To emphasize the word *light*, a logical choice was to flourish the ascender and descender. It worked well to balance them by moving in opposite directions with the tail of the flourish and conveniently crossing the *t* with the exit stroke of the ascender flourish.

Try it: Here are a few variations for you to trace, then take a few minutes to re-create them in your separate practice notebook. What's your favorite?

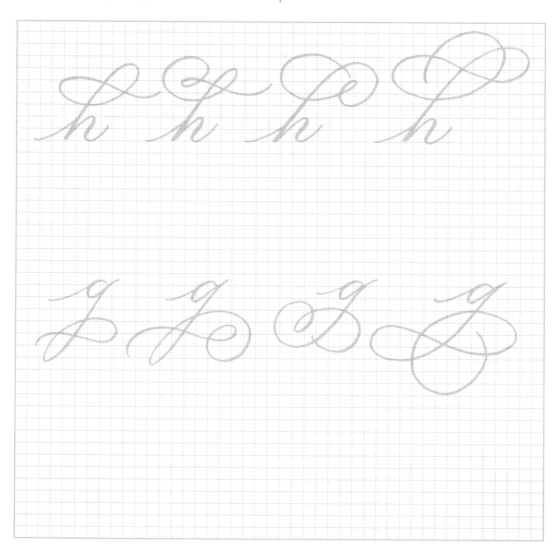

I AM HAPPY
TO BE ME
AND TO
SHARE MY

Light

WITH
OTHERS

Trace this design here, then re-create it in your own way on a piece of paper or in a frame at the back of this book.

Share Letter Strokes Creatively

Since this affirmation is about sharing, I wanted to demonstrate that concept through the letters sharing strokes. It's always a fine line to navigate between creative expression and clear legibility. Stacking the *A*'s worked well, and the diagonal strokes of the *M* naturally led to the *A*.

The *S-F* ligature and the double *O*'s also suggest sharing. Since it's difficult to center the text when you are prioritizing letter connections, you can use lines or some other pattern to create a unified and anchored overall appearance.

When you're working on a composition, take time to play with these serendipitous connections between letters. Be audacious in your ventures—even if it doesn't pan out for that particular use, you might be able to save it for another time!

Try it: Trace the *Sharing Happiness* portion of the affirmation, and then write it on your own in the blank area underneath.

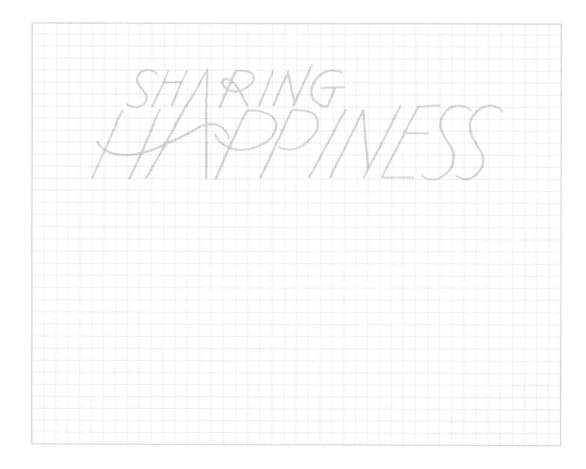

SHARING HAPPINESS WITH OTHERS HELPS ME FEEL HAPPIER TOO

Trace this design here, then re-create it in your own way on a piece of paper or in a frame at the back of this book.

Large, confident flourishing is one way to display the action and decisiveness that this quote suggests. Because the quote is shorter, there's plenty of room to go all-out on both the top and bottom. Here, it worked best to position the top flourish on the right, and the bottom one on the left.

Try this style of back-and-forth flourishing when it matches the vibe of the text or when you have extra space to fill.

Try it: Let's single out the y and h flourishes for specialized practice. These flourishes are written with a brush pen, while a monoline pen was used in the design. You can trace them with a brush pen or monoline tool to see which you prefer. Practice keeping your hand and wrist relaxed for smooth lines. You can write these flourishes in one stroke or, if you need a break to stop and reset, pause your pen at a cross section in the flourish to hide where you stopped and restarted.

Get out there and do what you love!

KARA GOUCHER

NOW IT'S YOUR TURN!

Trace this design here, then re-create it in your own way on a piece of paper or in a frame at the back of this book.

Practice Statement Letters with Filled Counters

When you have a message within your text that you'd like to accent in a fun and empowering way, hand-drawn letters with filled-in counters are an excellent skill to practice.

Filling in the counters of letters (as illustrated on page 36 in Part 1) is a bold way to make your message stand out. Here, with an internal theme pulled out of the larger quote, it helped to center every line. I decided to write the attribution line in a contrasting flourished script style to add elegance and contrast to the all-capital print design of the other lettering styles.

Try it: You can fill in counter letters completely with lines or with any other patterns. Fill in the empty row of counters however you'd like, then, in the space below the letters, draw your own counter letters and try a different filler.

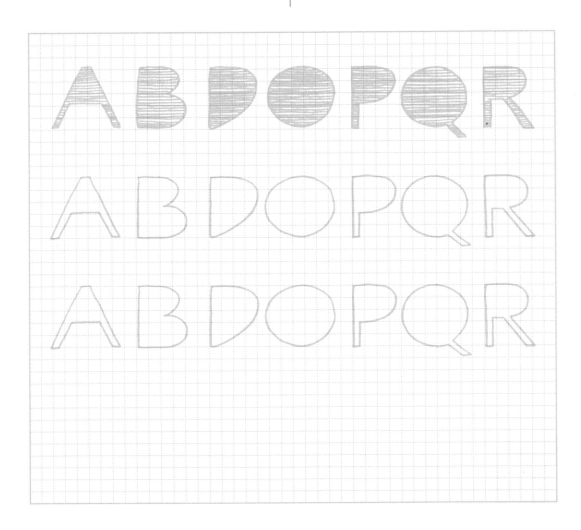

NO MATTER WHO
YOU
ARE, NO
MATTER
WHERE YOU
COME FROM,
YOU
ARE
BEAUTIFUL

Michelle Obama

Trace this design here, then re-create it in your own way on a piece of paper or in a frame at the back of this book.

Extend Letter Strokes in a Central Word

Letter extensions are a creative way to deepen the meanings of words and illustrations. The word *Happiness* was well suited to center stage here, with the rest of the text aligned on alternate sides. The snowflakes, with no two alike, illustrate the meaning of each day bringing unique delights. To accompany the snowflakes falling and swirling, I wanted the letters to also show action, reminiscent of tree branches swaying in the wind or a winter snow dance.

When you have a longer word, you can try to extend a letter stroke in all directions or do whatever looks best with your design. With a shorter word or busier design, you may find that only two extensions are needed.

Try it: You can make your extensions straight or wavy, as you see in these examples. Trace both words. Which do you prefer? Write the words again on your own in your practice notebook or experiment with writing some new words!

Every single day can bring me HAPPINESS in its own unique way

NOW IT'S YOUR TURN!

Trace this design here, then re-create it in your own way on a piece of paper or in a frame at the back of this book.

Make Capital Letters Take Center Stage

To emphasize words in a quote, it's a compelling design strategy to start these words with a capital letter. Here, you can keep the entrance strokes of the *B* and *Y* the same, as well as the *V* and *D* in the name of the quote's author. Repetitive themes like this are pretty, and they also give your designs a cohesive appearance.

When you have two or more capital letters, make them stand out by using a repeated entrance stroke. Refer back to the Creative Entrance Strokes practice exercise on page 48 in Part 1 for ideas.

Try it: Trace these capital letters with varied entrance strokes, then try your own in the blank spaces or in your notebook for further practice.

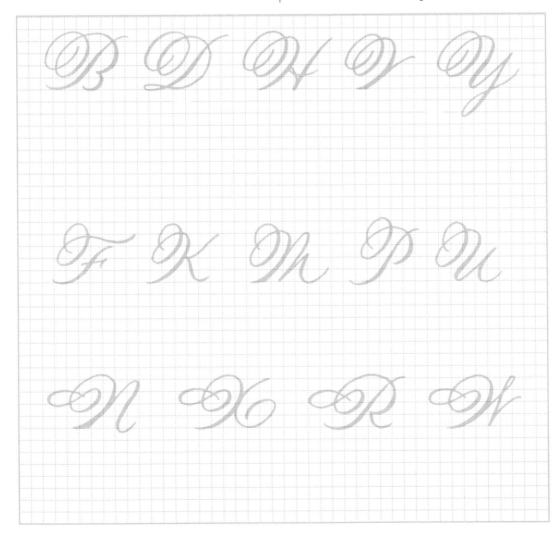

THE PRIVILEGE OF
A LIFETIME IS

Being

WHO

You

ARE

· *Viola Davis* ·

NOW IT'S YOUR TURN!

Trace this design here, then re-create it in your own way on a piece of paper or in a frame at the back of this book.

Lighten Up a Design with Simple Versals

Simple Versals (the full alphabet is shown on page 34) is incredibly personal and adaptable. The uneven lines here are meant to evoke the ups and downs of ordinary life. With the positive messages of beauty and laughter in bold, the "moody" lines take on an organic and rustic beauty reminiscent of water or rock. Letter joins, or ligatures, work exceptionally well with Simple Versals. Besides saving space, ligatures also give your design a human touch.

When you have other words that are easy to read, like the *and* and *something* shown here, you can use this technique of combining two letters into a ligature. You could also try crossing both the *g* and *h* in *laugh* or similar words with one bar, as shown here, instead of two. Sometimes this keeps your design cleaner and less clunky. Double *O*'s can often be linked together or drawn at half-size as shown here.

Try it: Trace these words in Simple Versals, especially noting ligatures that may be new to you, then practice writing the words again in the blank practice box.

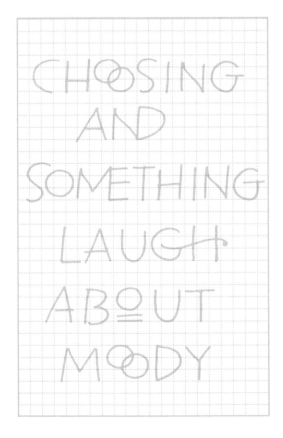

Trace this design here, then re-create it in your own way on a piece of paper or in a frame at the back of this book.

Connect Contrasting Lettering Styles

As you design, look for different ways to transition between lettering styles. Here, you can see some of the letter strokes that work well to connect and how adequate spacing keeps the design clean, balanced, and easily readable. The flourishes on the top and bottom are the same shape and are parallel to each other. It typically looks better to have the bottom flourish larger than the top to give the sense of a strong foundation.

When you are using more than one style of writing in your design, look for ways to connect one line to the next by flourishing off of ascenders, descenders, cross bars, and any other letter strokes that will connect in a way that looks natural and unforced.

Try it: To get the hang of the flow and spacing of these joins, trace these partial elements before working on the entire design. For further practice, choose a quote and practice similar connections in your notebook.

GIVE
BACK
IN SOME
WAY.
*Always
Be Thoughtful*
OF
OTHERS.
Jackie Joyner-Kersee

NOW IT'S
YOUR
TURN!

Trace this design here, then re-create it in your own way on a piece
of paper or in a frame at the back of this book.

Whimsy Print (see the full alphabet on page 32) is a great supporting style to enhance a highlighted word or phrase. Its unassuming presence helps to draw extra attention to the focal point in a design, and illustrations can also be a wonderful addition! Because this affirmation contains the word *surrounded*, encompassing the emphasized word *encourage* with budding leaves and berries is one fitting way to express meaning.

When you have one word or phrase you would like to stress, consider drawing around it to give it some extra love and attention. You can illustrate with whatever drawings best fit the meaning of your quote.

Try it: Trace these words to get more familiar with Whimsy Print, then rewrite them in the blank areas provided. Concentrate on upright strokes and consistent spacing between letters. You can also trace the bold capital letter examples of the *U-R* ligature and use a branch as a cross bar for a capital letter.

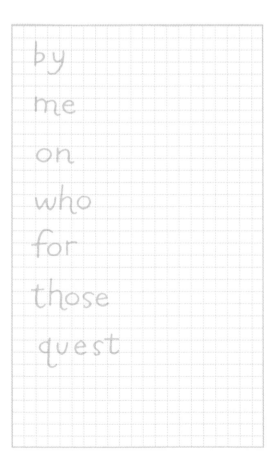

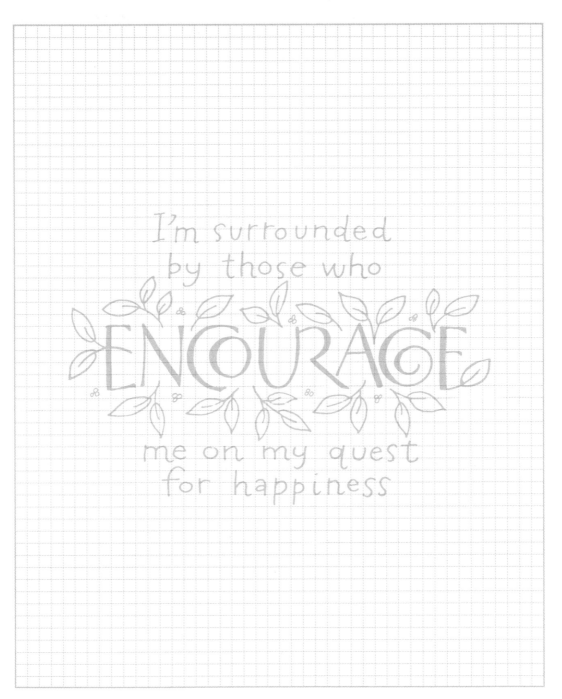

I'm surrounded
by those who
ENCOURAGE
me on my quest
for happiness

Trace this design here, then re-create it in your own way on a piece of paper or in a frame at the back of this book.

Incorporate Vintage Type Print Into a Design

Vintage Type Print (see the full alphabet on page 31) looks great on its own or used in multiple-style designs. As you can see here, it's tidy and legible without being stuffy, and it works well with illustrations.

Let's take a closer look at a few words to get the hang of the serifs and spacing of this fun style!

Try it: First, trace the words, then rewrite them in the blank practice boxes.

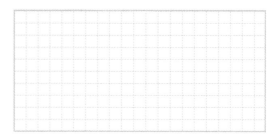

Go places.
Learn new stuff.

*Look
at the
World*

with wonder.

· A N G E L A   B A S S E T T ·

NOW IT'S YOUR TURN!

Trace this design here, then re-create it in your own way on a piece of paper or in a frame at the back of this book.

Try the Versatile Playful Script

Playful Script (see the full alphabet on page 25) is pleasant-looking and easy to read. It stands on its own or mingles well with both illustrations and other lettering styles. You can write it in monoline or with a brush pen—whatever your design calls for. Here, I penned the Playful Script in a lightweight monoline to give the botanicals an even spotlight.

Try it: Write some words, focusing on letter joins, consistency in slant, and even spacing between letters. Trace each word, then rewrite your own in the blank boxes.

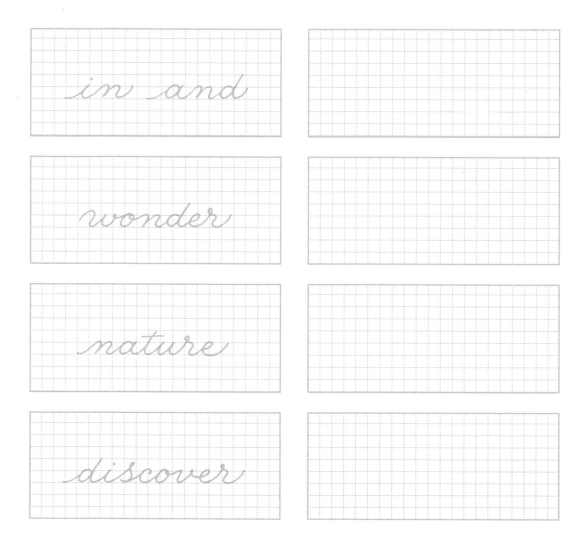

I discover wonder and delight through time in nature

NOW IT'S YOUR TURN!

Trace this design here, then re-create it in your own way on a piece of paper or in a frame at the back of this book.

Symbolize Genuine Letter Connection

Letter connections are a distinctive way to represent text. It takes a bit of time and patience to find letters that connect well and to work out spacing that looks good across different lines of text. In the following quote, the *I* and *U* and the *A* and *N* are attached to display the meaning of the text in a unique way that draws the observer in a little more.

The wavy lines serve to fit the whole text into a block that gives the design a cohesive look and an even shape. The attribution fits seamlessly into the wavy lines by extending the first and last letters of the name.

✎ **Try it:** Try connecting some letters. Names are a great way to practice this technique! Trace the example of my name, and then try yours in the blank space underneath to see if you can work out some letter connections. You can also try a friend's name, a phrase, or a favorite city and state.

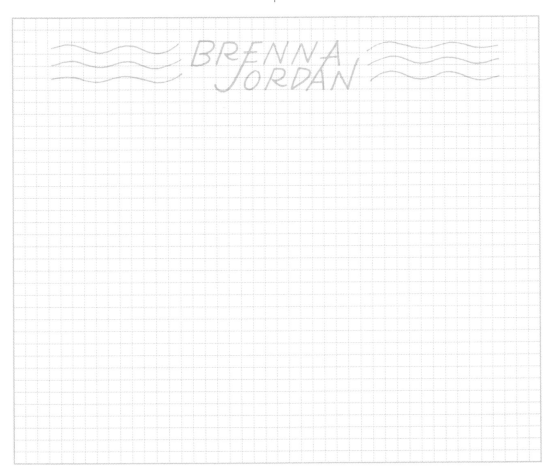

GENUINE
HUMAN
CONNECTION
*is more fulfilling
than anything that
technology has to offer*

—JON BATISTE

NOW IT'S YOUR TURN!

Trace this design here, then re-create it in your own way on a piece of paper or in a frame at the back of this book.

Draw Your Own Parallel Lines for a Longer Quote

When you have a longer quote that has a focal word near the center, you can give this technique a try. Spend some time working on spacing to figure out how long your lines need to be. Because the lines aren't rigid, you have a lot of flexibility to place words where you think they look the best.

Longer quotes require a little more work to fit all the text while still holding the interest of the reader. Here, the underline and overhead flourishes on the word *Happier* draw the reader into the theme of the quote. Drawing parallel lines to the flourishes instead of writing on straight lines helps to exhibit freedom, buoyancy, and a sense of movement and growth, which the text is exploring.

Most of the time, it's fairly easy to add these underline and overhead flourishes to your focus word. If you can't extend the first or last letter of the word, you can always use an unattached flourish.

Try it: Here's another example for practice, showing just the key word. Trace the word *Kindness* with an underline and overhead flourish, then trace the parallel lines above and below. In the practice space, rewrite *Kindness* or choose another word to create a similar image.

I'M CONFIDENT THAT TODAY'S CHALLENGES ARE GUIDING ME TO A *Happier* AND MORE RESILIENT, COMPASSIONATE, AND SELF-AWARE FUTURE

NOW IT'S YOUR TURN!

Trace this design here, then re-create it in your own way on a piece of paper or in a frame at the back of this book.

Emphasize Key Words with Empowered Print

Empowered Print (see the full alphabet on page 28) is an eye-catching way to emphasize key words in your design. Here, its tall, italicized stance gives it simple sophistication. Paradoxically, it stands out even though it is a lighter weight than the contrasting script.

When you're working on designs, Empowered Print is a solid option when you need your lettering to stand out and be read quickly. You can use it for headings in your bullet journal, stylish name labels, greeting cards, posters, and other signage.

Try it: Trace these words, then write your own in the blank practice boxes. Focus on uniform spacing between letters. It helps to try the trick of turning your page upside down to spot any holes or too-close spacing!

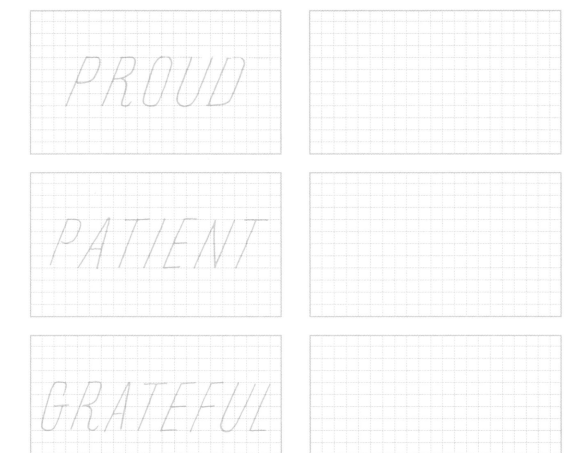

Today I am
GRATEFUL
for fresh
beginnings,
PATIENT
with my
progress, and
PROUD
of how far
I've come

NOW IT'S YOUR TURN!

Trace this design here, then re-create it in your own way on a piece of paper or in a frame at the back of this book.

Make Your Own Creative Border

When you'd like to accent your text with a simple border, try fitting this one into your design. You can freehand the line or use a ruler, then add a row of beads or other small illustrations to polish it off! You can also find more extensive full-page border and frame ideas in Part 3 of this book.

Using just one style while emphasizing significant words in all caps is a dynamic way to design a quote, and it works well for this longer one. The leaves fill in the blank places that were purposefully alternated on the left and right. The border gives the quote a charming finishing touch that fits the whimsical appearance of the rest of the design.

Try it: Letters with diagonal strokes extend into a loop, then a line. Here are a few words and borders to trace. Then, in the blank space below each word, rewrite the words and borders, and feel free to explore your own ideas for border illustrations.

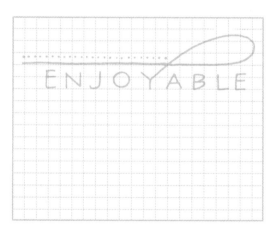

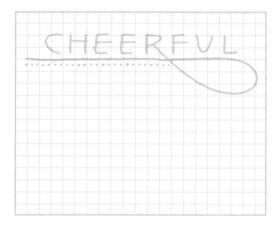

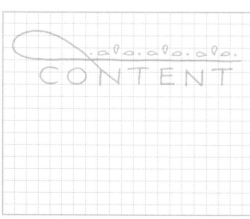

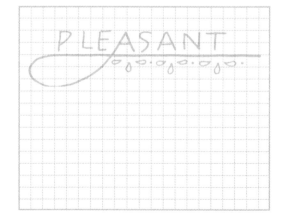

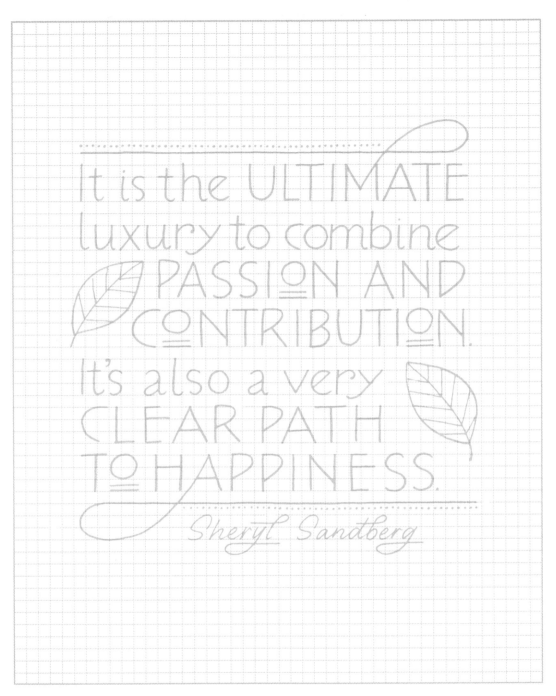

It is the ULTIMATE luxury to combine PASSION AND CONTRIBUTION. It's also a very CLEAR PATH TO HAPPINESS.

Sheryl Sandberg

NOW IT'S YOUR TURN!

Trace this design here, then re-create it in your own way on a piece of paper or in a frame at the back of this book.

Create a Side-by-Side Design with a Divider Between

When a quote has two parallel phrases, one layout method is to create them side by side in two contrasting styles. Here, both phrases were about the same size, so it was relatively easy to balance the two sides. During a walk, I spotted this grassy weed and brought home two stalks to draw as the divider. When you need inspiration, the outdoors is a great place to go!

Quotes with these kinds of parallel statements are ideal for this side-by-side approach. Make sure the columns are set up so there is no question about reading the text in the correct order. There may be times when you want to emphasize one statement and make that side of the text larger or embellish it with flourishes. You may also find a fitting illustration that works exceptionally well as a tall divider between the two texts.

Try it: Finish the design started here, replicating the writing styles. You can personalize the words if you like, such as *I am exhaling fear, regret, anxiety,* or *I am inhaling love, gratitude, courage, peace,* or whatever words fit your current situation the best! Then draw in the divider shown in the final design or create your own.

I AM
EXHALING
ALL MY
STRESS AND
WORRIES

and
inhaling
happiness
and joy

NOW IT'S YOUR TURN!

Trace this design here, then re-create it in your own way on a piece of paper or in a frame at the back of this book.

Create a Side-by-Side Design with a Divider Between

Draw Two-Word Banners Using Only Straight Lines

When you have shorter words in a quote, banners are an effective device for providing visual interest and ease of reading. When you have two banners in a design, you can vary where you place the fold. You can see that the first banner has the fold on the top right, while the second banner has the fold on the bottom left.

Try it:

Step 1. In your practice notebook, draw two horizontal parallel lines with pencil, then two more offset parallel lines.

Step 2. Draw two vertical lines and erase the line inside the banner.

Step 3. Close the ends of the banner with diagonal lines. Draw another diagonal line in the center for the fold of the banner, then write the words.

Step 4. Shade with quick strokes starting at the end and working toward the letters.

Try it:

Step 1. In your practice notebook, draw two horizontal parallel lines with pencil, then two more offset parallel lines.

Step 2. Draw two vertical lines and erase the line inside the banner.

Step 3. Close the ends of the banner with diagonal lines. Draw another diagonal line in the center for the fold of the banner, then write the words.

Step 4. Shade with quick strokes starting at the end and working toward the letters.

1.
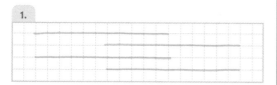

1.

2.
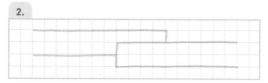

2.
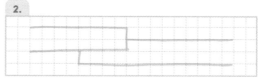

3.

3.

4.

4.

You MUST BE THE Best JUDGE OF YOUR OWN Happiness

JANE AUSTEN

NOW IT'S
YOUR
TURN!

Trace this design here, then re-create it in your own way on a piece of paper or in a frame at the back of this book.

Experiment with an Oval Design

An oval arrangement is optimal when the focal word is right in the middle of the quote. The smaller print is still relatively horizontal on the border of the oval and reads easily, and the flourish off the printed *y* in *actively* is similar to the flourish off the script *p* in *happiness*. To finish off the oval on the left and right sides, I added a flexible botanical that bends to create a finished shape!

When you're making your own layouts, experiment with some quotes that are well suited to this oval design. You can use this flourish sequence or experiment with other flourish fillers that catch your eye. Draw in illustrations to complete the oval if there are blank areas along the border.

Try it: Use a pencil to draft your own layout of a short quote within this oval, or freehand the affirmation on the right. Don't worry if you need to erase a lot; that's a vital part of the process!

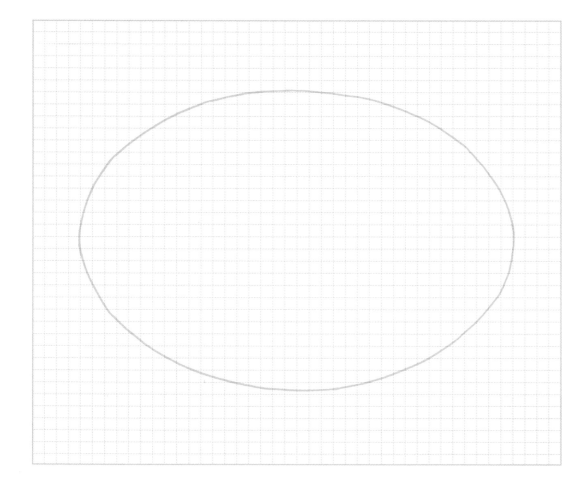

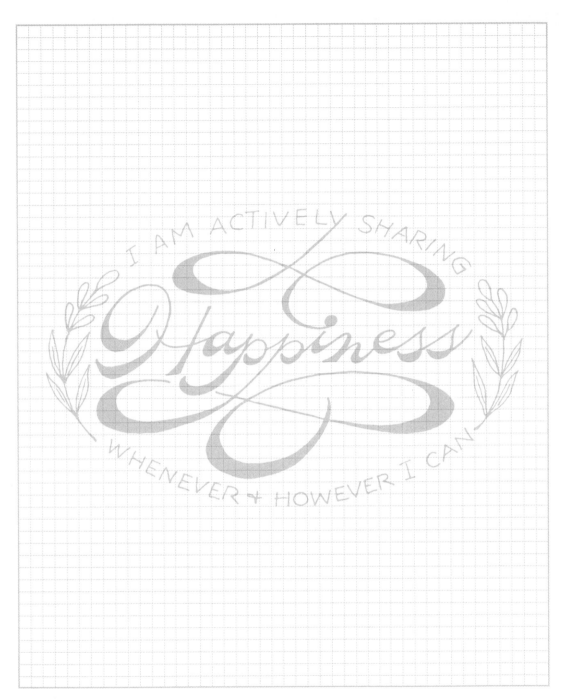

I AM ACTIVELY SHARING

Happiness

WHENEVER + HOWEVER I CAN

NOW IT'S
YOUR
TURN!

Trace this design here, then re-create it in your own way on a piece of paper or in a frame at the back of this book.

Try Overlapping Figure-8 Flourishes

When space is a concern but you want to add a little decoration, this small-scale flourish is a great one to pull out! This example consists of three ovals, but you can modify the flourish to have more or fewer. Because this is a longer quote, there wasn't room for super-big flourishes, but the *N*'s were perfectly positioned for some tighter, overlapping flourishes that point neatly back toward the design.

Try it:

Step 1. In your practice notebook, draw the outer lines of the *N*, then start at the top and draw the middle stroke and two ovals.

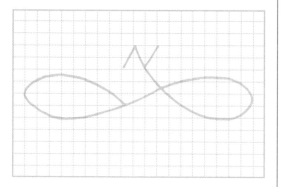

Step 2. Starting at the junction where you left off, draw the third oval and wrap around to end somewhere near the center of your left-hand oval.

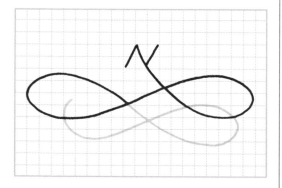

Try it:

Step 1. Now let's repeat these two steps to reverse the ovals and create an overhead flourish. In your practice notebook, draw the outer lines of the *N*, then start at the bottom and draw the middle stroke and two ovals.

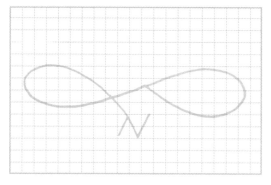

Step 2. Starting at the junction where you left off, draw the third oval and wrap around to end somewhere near the center of your right-hand oval.

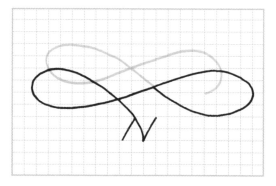

WHEN YOU
RELINQUISH
THE DESIRE
TO CONTROL
YOUR FUTURE,
YOU CAN HAVE
MORE
HAPPINESS

· NICOLE KIDMAN ·

NOW IT'S
YOUR
TURN!

Trace this design here, then re-create it in your own way on a piece
of paper or in a frame at the back of this book.

Use Simply Timeless Print to Support Focal Words

Simply Timeless Print (see the full alphabet on page 30) is a great choice when you need a style to play a supporting role and not distract from the focal words. Here, you can see the variation of Simply Timeless in a slanted rather than upright position. You'll see Simply Timeless Print in the banners as well. It's a go-to style for readability, and the size can easily be modified to fit the width of the banner. The script here spells out the theme of the quote "Happiness is Love" by using bold brush script.

Try it: Let's try this style alone and then within a banner to get some practice with these versatile letters. For extra practice, you can also try them with serifs. Trace the words, then write your own in the blank boxes. Concentrate on consistent slant and even spacing. Then follow the four steps in your practice notebook to create a banner containing words in Simply Timeless Print.

1.

2.

3.

4.

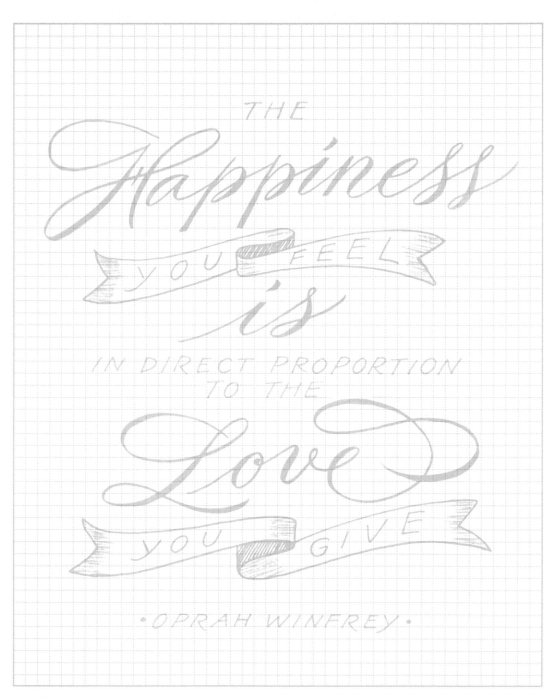

THE
Happiness
YOU FEEL
is
IN DIRECT PROPORTION
TO THE
Love
YOU GIVE

· OPRAH WINFREY ·

NOW IT'S YOUR TURN!

Trace this design here, then re-create it in your own way on a piece of paper or in a frame at the back of this book.

Attach Triple-Oval Flourishes to Your Letters

This design is a bit more complex to use because you need just the right combination of letters to make it happen. Look in your text for diagonal strokes in letters that extend in the directions you need and see if you can center the letters to create a balanced flourish. If it's hard to attach a flourish on both the top and bottom, you can modify to attach just one triple-oval flourish in either space.

This quote worked well to have attached triple-oval flourishes act as the main character. With the entire design centered throughout, the quote itself resembles a sign, and the triple ovals tie everything together. With a lot of rough-draft sketching, the diagonal strokes came together to make an even pattern on both the top and bottom.

Try it: Trace some of these letters that work for attaching triple-oval flourishes. For more practice, use your notebook and experiment with other letters with diagonal strokes.

MY EMOTIONS
ARE SIGNPOSTS-
I am curious
about them
AND WHAT THEY
ARE TELLING ME.

NOW IT'S
YOUR
TURN!

Trace this design here, then re-create it in your own way on a piece of paper or in a frame at the back of this book.

Use Spencerian Script in a Design

When you have a design with a large illustration, consider using Spencerian Script (see the full alphabet on pages 20–21) for the text. It is easy to read and blends well with artwork. With this script, you can cross the *t*'s in a wavy line above the stem, but for legibility, I prefer to cross them as demonstrated in this quote.

Since the focal point is the violin illustration, the straightforward Spencerian Script was a good match for this project. With the violin positioned diagonally, alternating the script on either side of the page helped balance the layout. The weight of the lettering is a little darker than the illustration, which also provides a balanced appearance.

Try it: Trace the words in the practice boxes, then rewrite them in the blank boxes.

Happiness
is a thing
to be

practiced,
like the
violin

—JOHN LUBBOCK

NOW IT'S YOUR TURN!

Trace this design here, then re-create it in your own way on a piece of paper or in a frame at the back of this book.

Fill Up a Circle Design with Flourishing

This flourishing skill typically works best with shorter quotes when the word you want to dramatize is in the middle of the quote. The supporting words can either be centered or offset (as seen here) on the outer rim of the circle shape. First, write the word in the middle of your circle. Then play around with flourishing the capital letter. Feel free to make several renditions of flourishing the blank areas until your design looks balanced. Have fun with the process!

This short quote, with the key word in the center, was a great option for a circle design. Flourishing off the end of

the word to cross the *t* was a reasonable way to fill the top part of the circle. But with no descenders in the word, I needed to create this unattached flourish to fill the bottom half. The flourishes on the capital *P* have similar elements as the top and bottom to help tie the whole design together.

Try it: Trace the Fancy Capital *P* before writing your own in the blank box, starting at the numbered arrows. Then trace the unattached flourish and write your own.

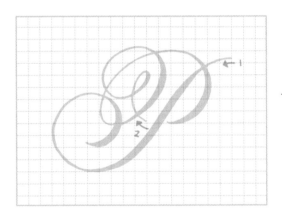

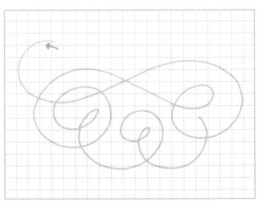

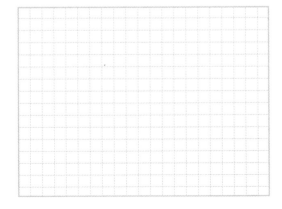

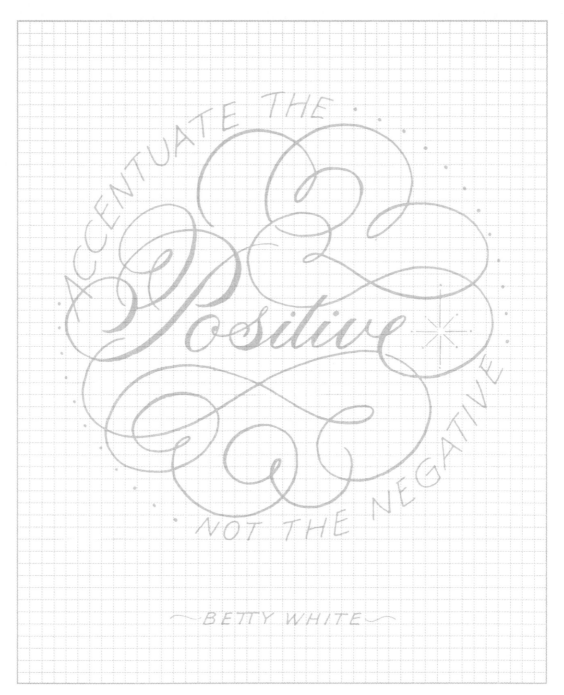

ACCENTUATE THE *Positive* NOT THE NEGATIVE

~BETTY WHITE~

NOW IT'S YOUR TURN!

Trace this design here, then re-create it in your own way on a piece of paper or in a frame at the back of this book.

Use Romantic Script in a Design

Romantic Script (see another example on page 41) is great for adding both beauty and contrast to a design. I like to use it for just a word or two rather than a whole design since it's an involved process to write and is easier to read in small doses. Here, it pairs well with Vintage Type Print and some cheerful flowers.

Try it: Trace the outline of *Happy* to get a sense of how the letter strokes relate to one another. Then have fun planning your own unique composition! Illustrate the word with flowers or whatever else you'd like to draw. Feel free to use colored pencils or markers, sparkle or gel pens, glitter, or other favorite materials.

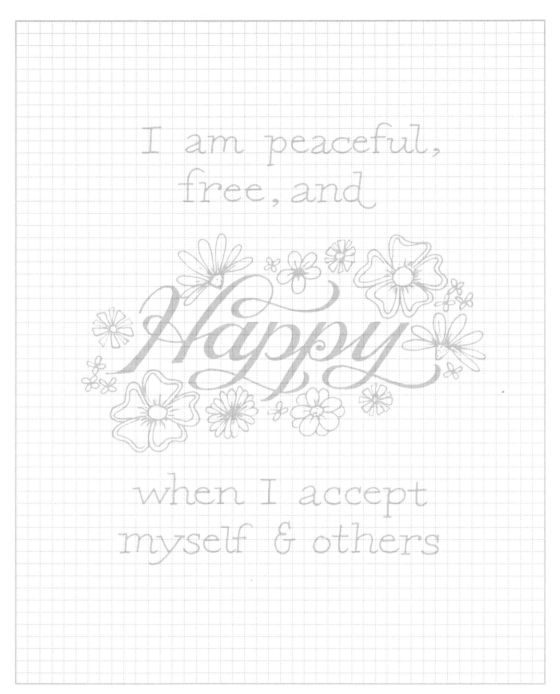

I am peaceful,
free, and

Happy

when I accept
myself & others

NOW IT'S
YOUR
TURN!

Trace this design here, then re-create it in your own way on a piece
of paper or in a frame at the back of this book.

Align Right and Left Sides of Your Lettering

You can try aligning the text of quotes in a couple of different ways. You may choose to center the text and add lengtheners on both ends or alternate the flourishing. Whatever method you choose, the process will take some persistence. Remember that every draft is a stepping stone to your final design, and ideas you don't use right now might come in handy later.

This quote has ten words, and after several different draft ideas, I decided to see what happened when I wrote two words on each line and worked to align both the left and right sides. Since the lines were different lengths, I had to find ways to stretch out the shorter lines through flourishing and strategic placement of the the attribution. Looking for places within the text to fill in space is also a great way to bring interest to a design with one lettering style. I thought it still needed something, so I added a simple border to the top and bottom as a finishing touch.

Try it: Practice some right-side alignment by finishing each line of the quote and ending as close to the line drawn as possible. You can replicate the flourishes shown here or create your own.

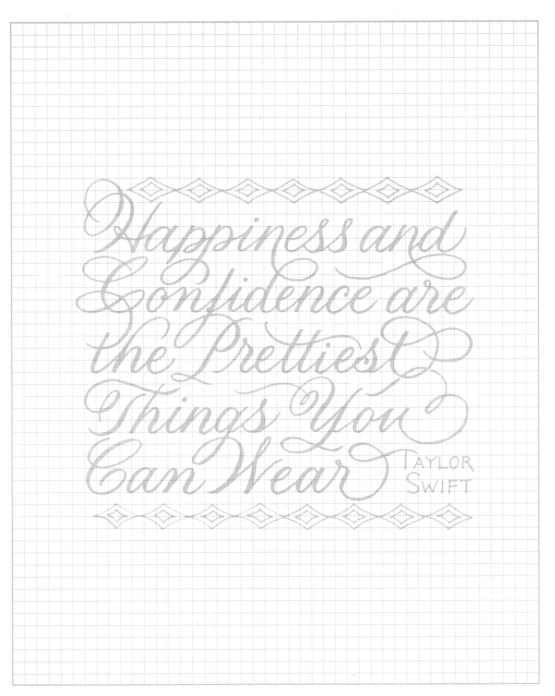

Happiness and Confidence are the Prettiest Things You Can Wear

TAYLOR SWIFT

NOW IT'S YOUR TURN!

Trace this design here, then re-create it in your own way on a piece of paper or in a frame at the back of this book.

Use Bold Alphabet for Emphasis

The Bold Alphabet (shown on page 38) is an appealing choice for a word you want to showcase, plus it pairs well with other styles and is easy to shade! When you have plenty of other elements in a design, this sans serif alphabet keeps things strong yet simple.

There are two focal words in this design, but to keep things interesting, they are in two different styles, Statement Letters and Bold Alphabet. Both words contain open letters with shading, but the thickness of the letters is different, and *Happiness* is written in an arc. Drawing one simple illustration to stand in for the O in *Loved* alludes to the uniqueness of each flower and helps to illustrate the meaning of the text.

Try it: First, trace the word, then add the shading. In the space below each word, try writing the letters on your own, concentrating on the varying thicknesses of the letter strokes.

The Greatest
HAPPINESS
of life is the
conviction
that we are
LOVED

Victor Hugo

NOW IT'S YOUR TURN!

Trace this design here, then re-create it in your own way on a piece of paper or in a frame at the back of this book.

Flourish a Shape Around a Design

One of the definitions of the word *cultivate* is "to promote or improve the growth of," so in this design, I wanted the letter strokes to show unfolding and expansion. I chose to write the text in monoline and emphasize the flourishing by shading only the curves on the outer edges. The shape of a diamond looked the best with this particular quote, but you can incorporate other shapes into your flourished designs.

If you use this technique with your text, sketch in pencil the shape that works the best with your layout. Work your way around using the letter embellishments to create a balanced design. It will take many drafts for the flourishes to all "get along," so be patient, keep a sense of humor, and take a break if you need to step away. Often fresh inspiration comes after time away.

Try it: Let's isolate a few unfurling elements and give them some extra practice to prepare for writing the whole design. Trace the word and add the shade. Then re-create it in the blank practice box.

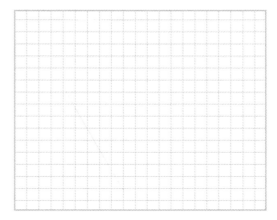

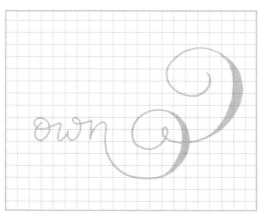

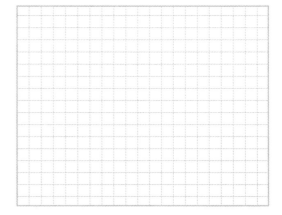

Every day you have to choose to find and cultivate your own happiness

·REESE WITHERSPOON·

NOW IT'S YOUR TURN!

Trace this design here, then re-create it in your own way on a piece of paper or in a frame at the back of this book.

Make a Cheerful Design with Jubilant Alphabet

When you want to stress just one word or phrase with hand-drawn letters, Jubilant Alphabet is a stellar candidate to consider. It is both bold and cheerful, and it was an easy choice for emphasizing the word *Happiness* here. Even with the banner and flourishing, the weightiness of Jubilant letters makes the word a definite focal point. A whole quote in this alphabet would be a little too much, so I like to pair it with other styles to bring some contrast to its boldness. Here, I changed up each pair of double letters just slightly, using a terminal for one letter and leaving the other letter without.

Try it: Practice tracing these words to get the hang of the slant and thicknesses of the letters. Then, in the blank areas below the words, try hand drawing them on your own. If you'd like further practice, refer to the whole alphabet on page 40 and draw some more words in your notebook.

Some cause
HAPPINESS
WHEREVER THEY GO;
Others, whenever
they go

·OSCAR WILDE·

NOW IT'S YOUR TURN!

Trace this design here, then re-create it in your own way on a piece of paper or in a frame at the back of this book.

Create a Double-Diamond Design

If you want to fit your quote into a diamond (or other) shape, draw the shape first, then try to fit in the words. It may take several attempts or maybe a new quote! For a double-diamond design, create negative-space diamonds in a significant word you'd like to showcase.

For this long quote, using a diamond shape to outline the text is a great way to make it both intriguing and easy to read. After trying various rough drafts, the text fit best with four lines above and below the focal word *HAPPY*. To take the

diamond design a step further, I drew diamonds in the thick stem of all the bold letters and penned around them in ink, a technique of using negative space to create an image.

Try it: In the first box, trace the letters from the word *HAPPY* in the design, then draw your own in the blank space underneath. In the second box, try out some other letters. You can refer to the Festive Print on page 33 to draw even more letters in your practice notebook.

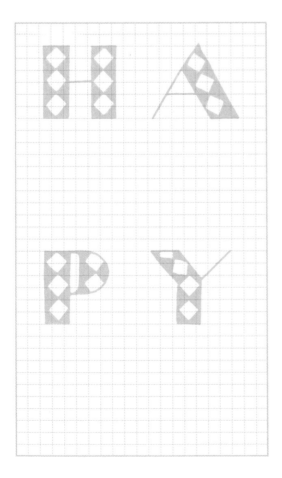

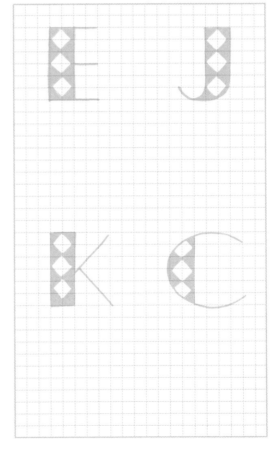

Be
healthy
and take care
of yourself, but be
HAPPY
with the beautiful
things that
make you,
you.

BEYONCÉ KNOWLES

NOW IT'S YOUR TURN!

Trace this design here, then re-create it in your own way on a piece of paper or in a frame at the back of this book.

Try a "Sandwich Flourish" for Your Design

When you have room in your design, large top and bottom flourishes help hold your text together. You can imagine them as being like the slices of bread that hold the filling of your sandwich or hamburger together. They are strong and foundational but also light and airy. To keep your piece balanced and cohesive, draw the flourishing on the bottom to either mirror or look similar to the top flourish.

Exuberant flourishing matched the tone and message of this hope-filled quote. Because there's a lot of repetition with the phrase *Never too late*, alternating two styles on every other line resulted in a design that's not too busy or monotonous. Using a brush pen for the repeated second and fourth lines added weight to help those words pop. The diagonal strokes of the *V* and the *A* were the perfect segue for composing joyful flourishes that "sandwich" the text.

Try it: Trace the top flourish to get a sense of the expansive movements of the loops and lines, then re-create both the top and bottom flourishes in your practice notebook. Feel free to invent your own unique twists and turns!

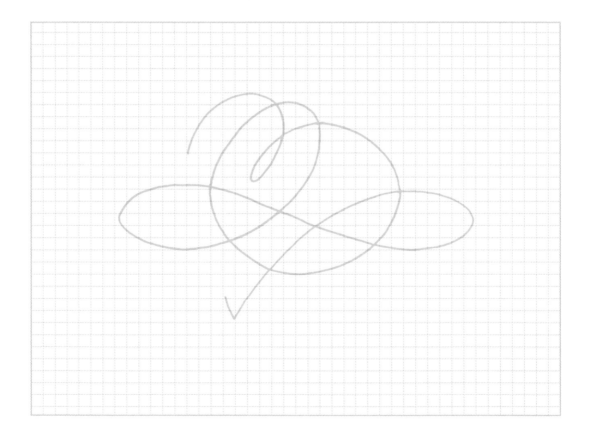

IT'S NEVER TOO LATE –
Never too late
TO START OVER,
Never too late
TO BE H·A·P·P·Y

JANE FONDA

Trace this design here, then re-create it in your own way on a piece of paper or in a frame at the back of this book.

Encircle Text in a Wreath

Since this quote alludes to the simple gifts surrounding us, I decided to encircle the text with a simple wreath in a nod to the beauty Anne Frank continues to give humankind through the legacy of her words. Since ancient times, the wreath has been a symbol of eternal life, so it seemed particularly fitting for this quote.

Try it: Turn this circle into a wreath by replicating the one used in this finished quote or adding whatever leaves, berries, pine branches, or elements from nature you'd like. When you've filled up your wreath, think of a word or two to script in the center. For further practice, trace a larger circle in your practice notebook to make a wreath, and select a short phrase to write inside.

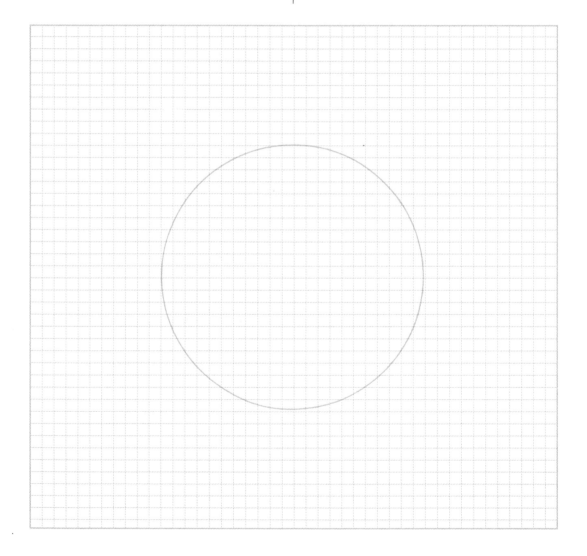

THINK OF

All the

Beauty

STILL LEFT AROUND
YOU AND BE
H·A·P·P·Y

·ANNE FRANK·

NOW IT'S
YOUR
TURN!

Trace this design here, then re-create it in your own way on a piece
of paper or in a frame at the back of this book.

Cross Two *T*'s in One Stroke

As you hand letter, you'll start to see double *t*'s as creative opportunities! When you work out an innovative way to cross two *t*'s in one stroke, have someone else look at the word to make sure it's easily deciphered. If they don't struggle to read it, and you love how it looks, you've got a keeper.

This quote was an extra-fun one to design because of the symmetry embedded in the word structure. With text like this, you can create almost a mirror image on the second half of the quote. Crossing both *t*'s in one stroke in the word *Gratitude* helped to accomplish this. The

main goal is to ensure that the stroke looks spontaneous. Here, it worked to use large oval-shaped curves to cross both *t*'s while also repeating some elements of the flourish on the bottom of the page. The rest of the design consists of very straight lines, so having these wide loops express joyful energy seemed to match the text's message.

Try it: Trace the word *Gratitude*. Then, in the space below the word, replicate the word and repeat this *t*-crossing or experiment with one of your own.

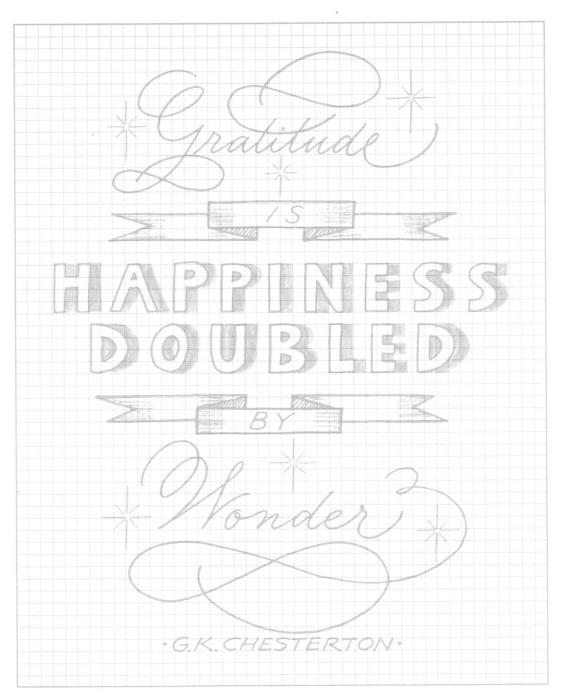

Gratitude is HAPPINESS DOUBLED by Wonder

·G.K. CHESTERTON·

NOW IT'S YOUR TURN!

Trace this design here, then re-create it in your own way on a piece of paper or in a frame at the back of this book.

Draw Curved Banners

Curved banners are conducive to many designs! You can use two, as shown here, to accent the center of a design, or simplify things and draw only one banner, arced in either direction.

In this design, banners with a slight arc help to turn the attention toward the emphasized phrase. The second banner is slightly bigger for aesthetics; it makes a design look stronger and more stable to have slightly more weight on the foundation.

eeel **Try it:** In your practice notebook, follow the sequence of the four steps shown to replicate a banner arced upward, then follow the four steps to make the banner curved downward.

1.

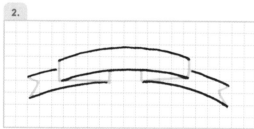

1.

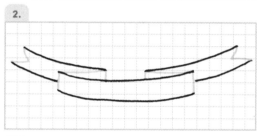

2.

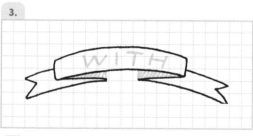

2.

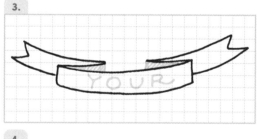

3.

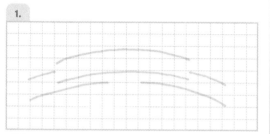

3.

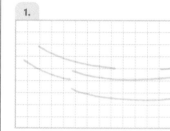

4.

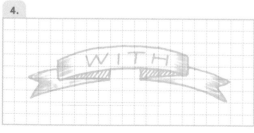

4.

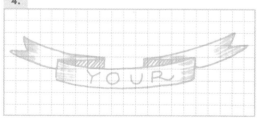

Be happy WITH being you. LOVE YOUR FLAWS. Own YOUR quirks.

—Ariana Grande

NOW IT'S YOUR TURN!

Trace this design here, then re-create it in your own way on a piece of paper or in a frame at the back of this book.

Flourish Around Your Lettering

After trying countless drafts with two contrasting lettering styles, choosing just one script style with surrounding flourishes seemed just right! Here, the gentle lines and generous loops of the flourishes demonstrate one interpretation of what an abstract concept like kindness could look like. The flourishes are written lightly in monoline to contrast the weightier brush lettering. You can also do the opposite by shading flourishes with monoline text (see the Flourish a Shape Around a Design project on page 128).

This type of all-out flourishing usually works best with shorter quotes with easily deciphered words. While you can definitely showcase pretty flourishing, you want to ensure that the message of the text isn't compromised. Be persistent with your design—even though flourishing looks easy and natural, it will take several drafts to get it to look the way you want.

Try it: In the finished quote, observe all the different ways these flourishes have been drawn: on capital letters, off of exit strokes, or unattached. Trace a few flourishes here to get loosened up, and then try to create your own.

Being Kind Always Works

·TOM HANKS·

NOW IT'S YOUR TURN!

Trace this design here, then re-create it in your own way on a piece of paper or in a frame at the back of this book.

Make a Scroll-Type Banner

Banners work great for longer quotes when you have a lot of supporting words in the text. This scroll banner tucks in neatly to the design, so it's especially advantageous in this piece with a lot going on.

In this design, I wanted to keep a rectangular shape for an easy flow when reading. It worked well to use straight lines to extend the supporting text lines since there were several pairs of small words. The banner was a solution for stretching across the whole space with just two short words, *to do*. The shading on the focal word *LOVE* and on the banners helps the two styles look like they belong together and makes the middle of the design stand out.

Try it: Starting with the first practice box, follow the sequence by drawing just the red lines with each step. Trace the final version in Step 7, then draw the whole banner, complete with shading, in Step 8. Use your notebook if you wish to make a larger scroll banner.

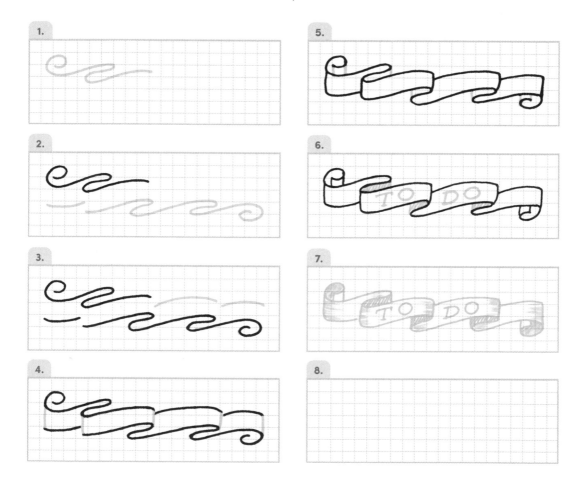

Happiness COMES FROM —
COMBINING
— WHAT WE —
LOVE
TO DO
— WITH —
SOMETHING
— THAT IS —
Meaningful
JAMES CLEAR

Trace this design here, then re-create it in your own way on a piece of paper or in a frame at the back of this book.

Create Illustrations Within a Circle Shape

Drawing illustrations within a circle almost creates the image of a portal into discovery, so it's great for projects about learning, growth, or breakthroughs. After I decided to highlight *Pursuing Happiness*, the rest of the text fit easily around it. Here, you can see that capitalizing the emphasized words showcases them even more. Filling in the space around the text with botanicals helps to illustrate one meaning of the affirmation—for you, it may be something entirely different!

Try it: Take a moment to read the words. You may even want to read them aloud and then close your eyes and think about what illustrations would best represent this affirmation for you. In the circle provided, sketch some of your ideas. If you'd like inspiration from the natural world, you may consider leaves, seashells, flowers, pine cones, berries, or other elements of nature. Make a larger "portal" in your practice notebook if you'd like more area for drawing.

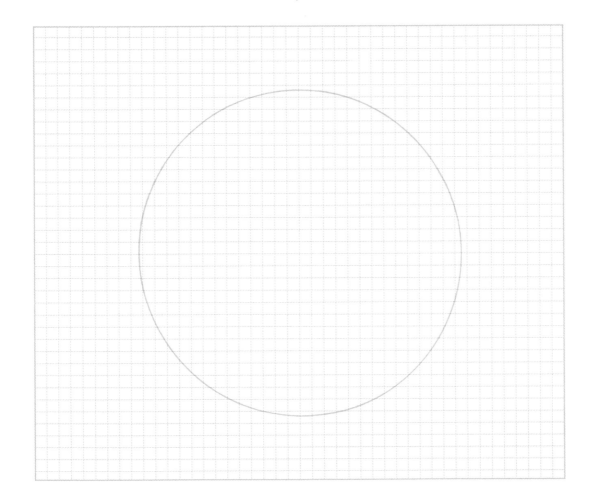

I'm intentional about *Pursuing Happiness* to uplift my mind, body, and spirit.

Trace this design here, then re-create it in your own way on a piece of paper or in a frame at the back of this book.

Create Illustrations Within a Circle Shape   147

Make Wavy-Line Extensions on Ascenders and Descenders

When you want an uncomplicated way to add motion and vitality to a layout, you can use this wavy line as an extension for both ascenders and descenders. It serves multiple purposes: It can showcase words, underline a design, fill up space, cross a *t*, or even become a stroke for another letter!

With a lot happening in this design, there wasn't space for large embellishments, but this simple wavy-line extension on the top and bottom added a clean finishing touch. These extensions don't compete with the rest of the design, but they do bring a sense of movement and energy to the piece.

Try it: Trace the words with the wavy-line extensions, then in the blank practice boxes, re-create your own. Try not to make the extension too straight; you want to keep just the right amount of gentle curvature to your line.

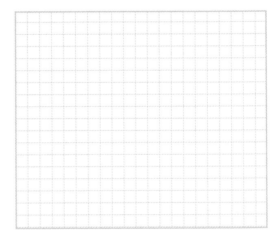

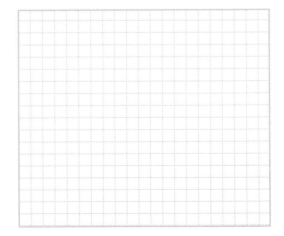

The happiness

OF · YOUR

L · I · F · E

depends on the

QUALITY

OF · YOUR

thoughts

· M A R C U S · A U R E L I U S ·

NOW IT'S YOUR TURN!

Trace this design here, then re-create it in your own way on a piece of paper or in a frame at the back of this book.

Use Illustrations to Convey Meaning

Illustrating the meaning of a quote helps bring the words to life! In this quote, I included some of my ideas of small treats, but you can use your own.

You can illustrate text to enhance your designs in many ways. Depending on the composition, you may want several drawings, as demonstrated here, or you may choose to keep it simple with just one or two images. Not only do illustrations help express meaning; they also pique interest to read (and remember) a message that may otherwise be overlooked. Consider adding illustrations to posters, signs, sticker designs, logos, banners, and your journal pages!

Try it: Trace the words, and then illustrate your favorite "small treats" in the blank area surrounding the words. You can even place the objects in front of you to look at while you draw them.

One of the
SECRETS
OF A
HAPPY
LIFE
IS
CONTINUOUS
Small
Treats

· IRIS MURDOCH ·

POP CORN

NOW IT'S
YOUR
TURN!

Trace this design here, then re-create it in your own way on a piece
of paper or in a frame at the back of this book.

Make an Ampersand Using Negative Space

When you have a lot going on in a design, particularly with multiple styles and many words vying for attention, an ampersand can save space and give an eclectic feel to a quote. You can add texture by enclosing the ampersand in a circle and filling in the space around it so the ampersand itself is the negative space left after inking around it. Depending on your design, you can form the words around the circle shape, as shown here with the word *laughter*.

꙳꙳꙳ **Try it:** Let's break this skill down into some steps. Trace each image in the four boxes. Then, in the blank space to the right of the examples, follow these steps.

Step 1. Outline a circle using a circle template (a coin or cap from something in your home works just as well if you don't have a template).
Step 2. Draw the ampersand, making the width fairly thick so it will stand out.
Step 3. Outline the ampersand in ink and carefully fill in the space around it. Voilà, a negative-space ampersand!
Step 4. Try another variation of an ampersand in the final practice box or draw your favorite style instead.

1.

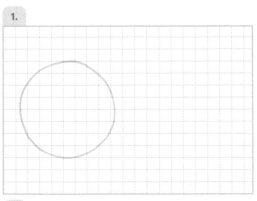

2.

3.

4.

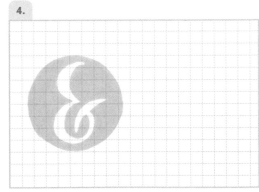

DETERMINE TO LIVE LIFE WITH Flair & LAUGHTER

♪♫ Maya Angelou ♫♪

NOW IT'S YOUR TURN!

Trace this design here, then re-create it in your own way on a piece of paper or in a frame at the back of this book.

Create a Multi-Style Design

This quote containing a lot of momentous words was the perfect candidate for a multi-style composition. Putting a lot of styles in one design is also an enjoyable way to practice what you are learning in a practical context. You have a chance to contemplate what styles fit best with what words and decide how to put them all together. When you are drafting your layout, draw lines in pencil on either side to keep the text in a "bookmark" shape.

Using a long, rectangular shape with one or two words per line keeps a layout like this one uncluttered and easy to read. The negative-space ampersand you learned previously is a good space-saving skill for these shorter lines.

Try it: Here are four of the styles you can trace and re-create. Think about how you can assimilate these styles into your own designs.

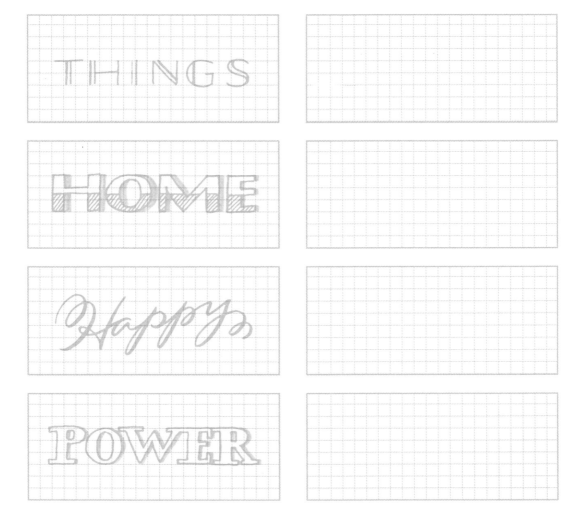

The
POWER
of finding
Beauty
IN THE
humblest
THINGS
m·a·k·e·s
HOME
Happy
& LIFE
Lovely
— LOUISA MAY ALCOTT

NOW IT'S YOUR TURN!

Trace this design here, then re-create it in your own way on a piece of paper or in a frame at the back of this book.

Frames for Your Projects

"Vision is the art of seeing what is invisible to others."
—Jonathan Swift

Now it's time to venture out and create on a blank canvas! These pages can be cut out and used to re-create any of the fifty projects from Part 2, or you can design your own favorite quotes and affirmations using the Seven Steps for Quote Designs on page 42. The pages can be framed to give as special gifts or to use for your own home decor as reminders of the power of hand lettering to spread happiness. Each image is made to fit a 5" × 7" frame. Before you begin, here are a few helpful tips to make the most of the frame pages:

- Sketch your design draft on tracing paper first. Then you can place it on top of the frame to easily determine if it fits well within the frame pattern before transferring it to the final page.
- Each of the sixteen frame designs is different. Consider repeating an element from the frame pattern somewhere in your design to tie the two together!
- Write your design on the frame page in pencil first to check for any errors, and then ink it in when you are satisfied with the layout.
- Use a ruler to achieve straight lines and more accurate spacing between lines.
- While creating your masterpieces, refer back to any of the alphabets, design elements, or previous projects to get ideas, and be on the lookout for inspiration around you.

Most importantly, look within yourself with great curiosity, acceptance, and confidence, and you will discover what you love to create and what makes you the happiest.

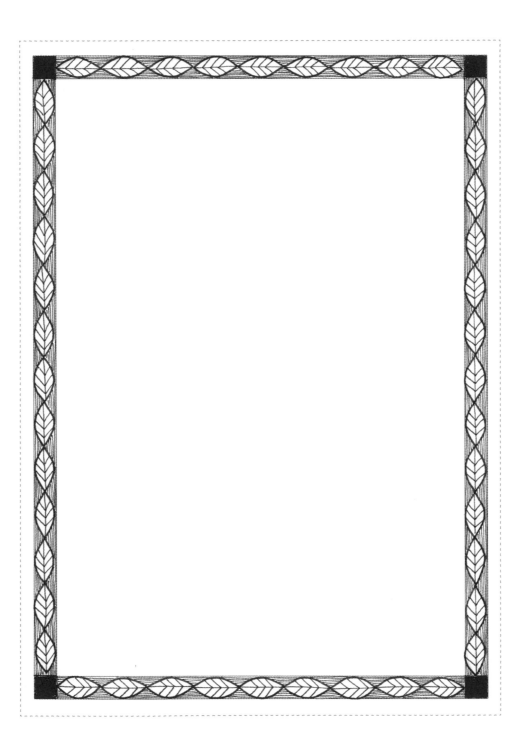

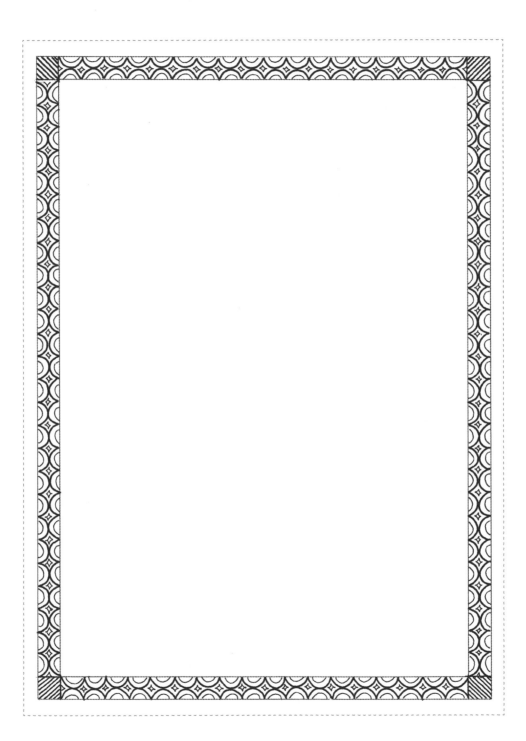

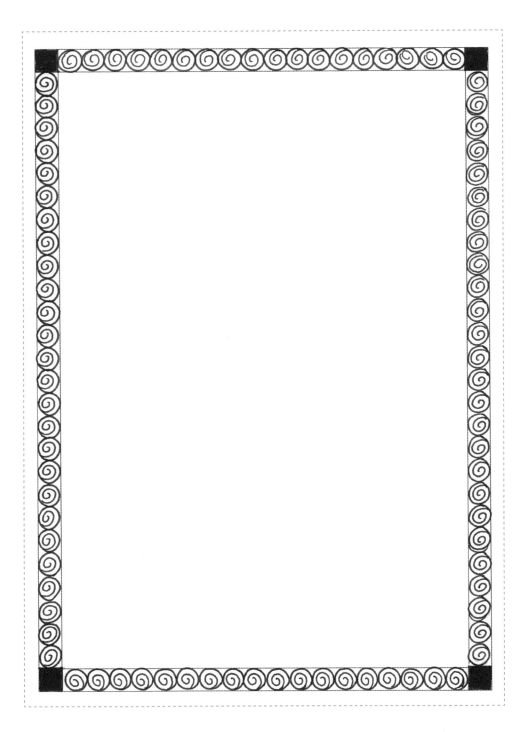

About the Author

"*The written letter is something personal, organic, unique, and spontaneous. It mirrors the character and the personality of the writer, and often his mood of the moment.*"

—Emil Ruder

Brenna Jordan is the author of *The Lost Art of Handwriting*. She has been exploring the art of lettering since receiving her first calligraphy pen in the sixth grade, and has studied with IAMPETH (International Association of Master Penmen, Engrossers, and Teachers of Handwriting) and The Colleagues of Calligraphy.

Brenna is known for her ability to meld traditional technique with modern flair. She offers customized calligraphy services through her studio, Calligraphy by Brenna, and especially enjoys unique calligraphy projects on less traditional surfaces such as rock, wood, leaves, and walls. She also loves hearing from her readers about how their experiences with writing by hand have been life-changing.

She lives in Duluth, Minnesota, with her family, and derives much of her inspiration and joy in creating from spending time in the beautiful outdoors. She enjoys running, skiing, and jumping in the chilly waters of Lake Superior. To learn more, visit BrennaJordan.com, along with her *Instagram* account, @calligraphybybrenna.

Explore the lost art of *writing* with fun prompts, worksheets, exercises—and more!

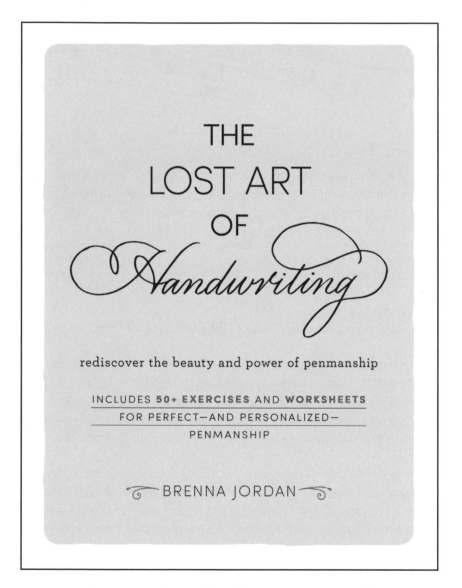

THE
LOST ART
OF
Handwriting

rediscover the beauty and power of penmanship

INCLUDES **50+ EXERCISES** AND **WORKSHEETS**

FOR PERFECT—AND PERSONALIZED—
PENMANSHIP

BRENNA JORDAN

Pick up or download your copy today!